THE BARCLAYS GUIDE TO

Managing Growth

in the Small Business

COLIN GRAY

BARCLAYS
Published by
 BLACKWELL

First published 1991

Basil Blackwell Ltd
108 Cowley Road, Oxford, OX4 1JF, UK

Basil Blackwell, Inc.
3 Cambridge Center
Cambridge, Massachusetts 02142, USA

British Library Cataloguing in Publication Data
A CIP catalogue record for this book is available from
the British Library.

Library of Congress Cataloging in Publication Data
Gray, Colin.
  The Barclays guide to managing growth in the small business/
Colin Gray.
  p. cm.—(Barclays small business series)
Includes bibliographical references.
ISBN 0–631–17249–1:
  1. Small business—Management. I. Title. II. Series.
HD62.7.G72 1991
658.02′2—dc20 90–20808 CIP

Typeset in 10½ on 12½pt Plantin
by Hope Services (Abingdon) Ltd
Printed in Great Britain by
T.J. Press Ltd., Padstow, Cornwall

THE BARCLAYS GUIDE TO

Managing
Growth
in the Small Business

Barclays Small Business Series

Series Editors: Colin Gray and John Stanworth

This new series of highly practical books aimed at new and established small businesses has been written by carefully selected authors in conjunction with the Small Business Unit of Barclays Bank. All the authors have a wide experience of the theory and, more important, the *practice* of small business, and they address the problems that are likely to be encountered by new businesses in a clear and accessible way, including examples and case studies drawn from real business situations.

These comprehensive but compact guides will help owners and managers of small businesses to acquire the skills that are essential if they are to operate successfully in times of rapid change in the business environment.

The Barclays Guide to Marketing for the Small Business
Len Rogers

The Barclays Guide to Computing for the Small Business
Khalid Aziz

The Barclays Guide to International Trade for the Small Business
John Wilson

The Barclays Guide to Financial Management for the Small Business
Peter Wilson

The Barclays Guide to Managing Staff for the Small Business
Iain Maitland

The Barclays Guide to Managing Growth in the Small Business
Colin Gray

The Barclays Guide to Franchising for the Small Business
John Stanworth and Brian Smith

The Barclays Guide to Law for the Small Business
Stephen Lloyd

The Barclays Guide to Buying and Selling for the Small Business
John Gammon

Contents

Foreword   ix

Acknowledgements   x

1 Introduction: the main problems facing the growing firm   1
  Lack of time   4
  Growth in confusion   6
  Overcrowding   8
  Low staff morale   10
  Weak financial records and cash management   11
  Summary   13

2 Identifying your own main growing pains   14
  Setting attainable goals   15
  Organizing for growth   18
  The demands of a growth market   22
  Controlling the process of growth   26
  Accommodating growth   28
  Summary   31

3 Finding time to plan   32
  Identifying your main time wasters   32
  Setting priorities   35
  Organizing the working week   36
  Managing information flows   38
  Summary   41

4 Developing the right team for growth   42
  Analysing your job requirements   43
  Structuring your organization   46
  Producing clear job descriptions   50
  Recruit or train?   53

Contents

Controlling your workforce 60

Maintaining motivation 64

Summary 71

5 Creating the space for growth 72

Auditing your premises needs 73

Efficient use of space 77

Refurbish or relocate? 79

Lease or buy? 81

Summary 83

6 Keeping your finances under control 85

Keeping track of your finances 86

Using financial information 91

Avoiding the pitfalls of overtrading 92

Financing your growth 97

Summary 103

7 Focusing on your growth products 104

Targeting growth customers 104

Researching markets and trends 108

Managing declining products 113

Developing new products 117

Summary 122

8 Developing your future growth strategy 124

Keeping ahead of your competition 125

Clearing the decks 130

Introducing information technology 136

The effects of the Single European Market 139

Developing your corporate culture 143

Summary 149

9 Removing future uncertainty through planning 150

Identifying preferred directions 150

Facilities for the future 152

Reviewing your organizational needs 154

Reviewing your training needs 155
Setting future business targets 157
Summary 158

Appendix: Sources of information 160

Supplementary reading 162

Glossary 164

Foreword

The last five years have seen a significant growth in the number of small businesses in all sectors of industry in the UK. Unfortunately they have also seen an increase in the numbers of problems encountered by those businesses. Often the problems could have been avoided with the right help and advice.

Barclays, in association with Basil Blackwell, is producing this series of guides to give that help and advice. They are comprehensive and written in a straightforward way. Each one has been written by a specialist in the field, in conjunction with Barclays Bank, and drawing on our joint expertise to ensure that the advice given is appropriate.

With the aid of these guides the businessman or woman will be better prepared to face the many challenges ahead, and, hopefully, will be better rewarded for their efforts.

George Cracknell
Director UK Business Sector
Barclays Bank plc

Acknowledgements

Ideas and experience do not spring from a void and I wish to thank some of the people whose own ideas, questions and criticisms have helped construct my awareness of small business reality. Most immediately, I would like to mention the stimulating ideas provided by the Council members of the Small Business Research Trust who collectively provide the widest range of opinions and small business experience in Britain – lobby groups, bankers, industrialists, academics, consultants and small business owners. More directly on the subject of small business growth, colleagues and various contributors to the national distance-learning Small Business Programme – as well as more than two hundred small business owners who kindly made available their personal experiences as teaching points in the various workbooks, video and audio cassettes – provided plenty of interesting food for thought.

On a more general level, I thank my fellow lecturers at the Open Business School at the Open University who constantly, if inadvertently, remind me that small businesses are not merely bigger businesses boiled down and that management problems change as businesses grow. Finally, anonymous mention should be made of the large number of owners and managers of smaller businesses (growers and otherwise) whom I have met and interviewed over the years, and, last but not least, the various creditors, VAT and Inland Revenue inspectors, the landlord and fate for not driving International Broadcasting Services out of business before giving me a couple of years of experiencing at first hand the dubious joys of unplanned growth.

The author and publisher would like to point out that the use of the masculine pronoun 'he' is not gender specific.

I

Introduction: the main problems facing the growing firm

Outline

Encouraging businesses to grow and promoting new businesses has been a policy feature of recent governments, but business growth cannot be turned on like a tap. Growth in business is usually not free from pain and the owners of smaller businesses have to address a number of problems associated with growth before they can develop their businesses successfully. These main problems are:

- the lack of time
- organizational confusion
- the lack of sufficient space
- absenteeism and low staff morale
- cash-flow problems
- no systematic approach to cash-flow management
- inadequate financial records
- loss of personal identity

Business growth has dominated economic debate in Britain for at least the past twenty years, and small businesses have occupied centre stage in that debate for the past ten. Although small business growth – both in terms of the number of firms and in terms of the expansion of individual firms – is generally regarded as a good thing, few commentators seem to realize that business growth for a small firm is no simple matter. Indeed, people who are not in business themselves are often surprised to learn that business growth can be regarded by business people as a not particularly pleasant experience. In fact, very few firms ever grow to any great extent, usually because their owners either never intend them to grow or because they prefer to avoid the growing pains. The basic purpose of this book is to take the pain out of growth by helping the managers of smaller firms to identify the cause of any growing pains, and by exploring how to adopt a simple, planned approach in overcoming the problems of growth.

The advice in this book is based on the assumption that you are the main decision-maker (either the owner or the manager) in a new business or in a small firm which is beginning to expand, and that you are experiencing some problems or surprises that you had not anticipated. Indeed, you may have bought this book because your previous growth now seems to have unexpectedly tailed off. This almost certainly means that your growth is unplanned even though it may not be unintended. Your business may be growing because your local economy is expanding, or because it is in an industry which is fairly dynamic, or because you feel that your business needs to be bigger to be more credible or to provide you with a sufficient income. If your business has started growing because of persistent strong demand, you are, of course, very fortunate, but you will need to make sure that you are managing the growth in the most efficient way possible. Many less fortunate, new smaller businesses are in overcrowded or stagnant industries and find it hard to grow.

Of course, even if your business is in one of these industries of relative non-growth, you can still manage to grow. However, it is likely that you have had to put a lot of effort into improving your product and increasing the output of your business. You may have neglected other aspects of your business which now require attention. In relation to the neglected areas, your growth will have also been unplanned. The aim of this book is to explore each of the important areas of your business so that you can decide on the most appropriate way for you to allocate your time, attention and resources to achieve balanced growth. The first three chapters deal directly with the common problems of growth experienced by smaller and newer firms, the next four chapters analyse the key issues of planning for growth, and the final two chapters examine the main elements of future growth strategies.

The immediate aim of this chapter is to explore more closely the common problems associated with unplanned or unanticipated

	Yes	No
Please answer the following questions by ticking the appropriate box.		
1. Have you recently found that you virtually never have time to complete all the tasks that you have set yourself to do each day?	☐	☐
2. Do you find that you never have enough time to sit down and work out where your business is heading?	☐	☐
3. Are members of your staff complaining that they do not have enough time to complete their jobs satisfactorily?	☐	☐
4. Are members of your staff increasingly complaining that other members of staff have not been doing their jobs or else have been trespassing on jobs that are not theirs?	☐	☐
5. Have you found that important jobs are being left undone or forgotten?	☐	☐
6. Do you suspect that not every person in your business is clear about what job he is responsible for?	☐	☐
7. Are members of your staff complaining that people are working on top of each other and that they do not have enough room to do their jobs properly?	☐	☐
8. Have you been losing staff or has staff absenteeism been increasing to the extent that you are finding it hard to fulfil your orders?	☐	☐
9. Have your orders increased without any increase of your cash balances or profits?	☐	☐
10. Do you feel that your business has changed and that you have lost touch with your staff?	☐	☐

Exhibit 1.1 The main problems of growth

growth. Exhibit 1.1 summarizes the main points and can help you monitor these problems as your business continues to grow.

Clearly, if you answer YES to all ten questions, you are facing a serious case of unplanned growth and your priority must be to find enough time to analyse the main cause of your problem and take some immediate action. Only in this way will you have more time to plan a longer term solution. If, on the other hand, you feel that you can honestly answer YES to only one of the questions, then you may only need to turn to the relevant chapter in this book to see if the solution to that problem lies there. Not surprisingly, the most commonly mentioned problem is the big complaint of virtually all smaller businesses (whether growing or not) – the lack of time. This is closely followed by the problem of increased confusion – too many crises, no clear lines of responsibility, the difficulty of keeping track of things, persistent problems ignored, letters unanswered and not knowing exactly what other people are doing. And, of course, there are the physical problems of overcrowding and lack of space. To some extent, however, these problems may be symptoms of an underlying shift in the nature of your business and may be treated as early warning signals. If you are growing, it may be that you should be moving towards a more structured approach to managing your business.

Indeed, there are other types of problems which are more obviously connected to how you organize or manage your business. Businesses that have been experiencing unplanned growth for some time often notice an increase in absenteeism and high staff turnover. The financial records are usually in a mess and invoices may be falling behind. Even worse, it may be that your output and workforce have actually increased but that you are running out of cash or your profits may have fallen. In fact, if you are suffering from unplanned growth, you are likely to be experiencing several of these problems at once and it may be difficult for you to put your finger precisely on the main problem and you may even feel that you are out of control. Fortunately, finding a solution is within your control. The clue to doing so lies in analysing your growth problems to reveal the areas of your business that are peripheral to your own real business goals. Each of these growth problems will now be examined in more detail.

Lack of time

As your business grows, you should set aside more time to assess where you are and to plan your future. Unfortunately, time is always in short supply in smaller businesses, especially when they are growing. The reason why finding enough time is often a problem in smaller businesses is that there are so many different ways of wasting and losing time. In most businesses, big and small, the biggest time wasters are usually interruptions that are allowed to crowd out other jobs. Interruptions come in many guises – telephone calls, talkative colleagues, customers with minor (but not major) complaints, queries from your bank manager, people trying to sell you their goods or services, and so on – and every manager has to develop an effective system for dealing with them. Another common time waster is travel. Every time you have to go somewhere, even if only to and from work, you use up time. Obviously, if you – or your key members of staff – spend a great part of the working day selling, or visiting potential clients, suppliers, sources of finance and the like, then travel is absorbing an enormous amount of productive time.

For most of these common time-management problems there are simple antidotes. For instance, getting an early start in the morning means that you can avoid phone calls, personal visitors and social chit-chat and get stuck into work for a couple of highly productive hours each day. Also, if you do not yet have a secretary, make sure that the one you hire is someone confident enough to screen all your incoming phone calls and visitors. If you already have a secretary, make sure that everybody knows that you prefer your messages to come via him or her. However, you will not be able to use your secretary to avoid time lost to travel, so you should make sure that you always have some reading material related to your work or market with you (or audio cassettes if you are driving) so that you can make use of your travel time. There are also a number of other techniques that you can use but remember that these are only limited solutions which do not go to the heart of the time-management problems caused by your unplanned growth.

Question 1   What is your own most common time waster?

It is likely that you have managed to identify more than one common time waster and, once you have identified them, you are more likely to be on guard. However, there are likely to be other time wasters that may not be so obvious. The main practical methods of effective time management are discussed in chapter 3. For the moment, it is sufficient to point out that most time is wasted because people allow themselves to become absorbed by tasks that are relatively unimportant. In a smaller business, the problem is usually worse because many small business owners have a tendency to take on too many tasks and to try to control the detail of other people's tasks instead of concentrating on their own, more important ones. Which tasks are important for you, of course, depends very much on your own business goals. As you work through this book, many of the suggested solutions to the problems of growth will have a direct impact on how you organize your time and how you organize your business.

Growth in confusion

The next most obvious feature of unplanned growth – after lack of time – is the increase in general confusion over what everybody should be doing. This is clearly an organizational problem for which you will require some time for planning. In part, the problem of doing too many overlapping jobs arises because nobody has a clear idea of their precise duties and responsibilities. Again, the fundamental cause of this problem is that in the early days of a business most people have to be able to do most jobs. If growth catches you unawares, you will find that most of your original staff, and many newcomers, will continue trying to do a wide range of jobs. As your volume of orders increases, it is inevitable that some orders will be duplicated and that some orders will get missed out altogether. You will begin to hear complaints that nobody knows what they are supposed to do. Also, you will find that many of the difficult or the more boring (but necessary) jobs will not get done at all.

Unless you and your staff have a clear idea of your and their various duties and responsibilities, growth will lead to your losing more money, staff and customers, as well as time. Just as you need to sort out your own priorities to manage your use of time, so too do you have to work out the job priorities of your key members of staff. In deciding those priorities, there are two important considerations to take into account. First, you have to have a clear idea in your own mind about your own personal business goals, so that you know the direction in which you would like to lead your business. Secondly, your staff will have their own ideas about each other's relative strengths and where they think their jobs are headed. Because your key staff have been intimately involved with the growth of the business, you should involve them as you refine responsibilities and clarify their job descriptions.

Question 2   Who are your key staff? What are the areas in which their duties or responsibilities overlap?

Basically, your objective should be to agree a set of duties and responsibilities for each member of staff, so that overlaps are minimized and the completion of each important task in your business is the clear responsibility of one person (including setting yourself a set of clear responsibilities and priorities). The techniques and issues connected with reorganization, including how to successfully delegate tasks and authority, are covered in detail in chapter 4. For the moment, the important point to understand is that any strategy for overcoming the effects of unplanned growth will involve reorganization. Furthermore, reorganization is not a static one-off solution but an ongoing dynamic process. As your business continues to grow or develop, you will constantly need to reassess how your business is organized. Indeed, most planning is about making sure that your business is organized appropriately to deal with anticipated changes or demands.

Of course, the success of this reorganization of your business will be more likely the closer the views of your key members of staff are to your own goals for your business. However, if you come across some opposition or a clear divergence of objectives, then you will have isolated one of the causes of your growth problems. If you do have such a problem, then you have only two options. Either you discuss the problem and come to an agreement, or you have to part company. These issues, particularly the second option, are discussed in chapter 9. The manager of a small business has to have a clear idea of its products and markets and cannot afford the luxury of too many conflicting views at an early stage if the business is to grow successfully.

For example, if you have a small engineering factory – which we can call Batchjob Ltd – and you have been expanding as a result of a growing number of small-batch contracts, but you discover that your production supervisor prefers doing longer-term sub-contracts producing single components for larger manufacturers, then you have a real difference in outlook which could be dangerous to your ultimate plans and the stability of your business. Similarly, the owner of a computer bureau (say, Compburo Associates), who believes that consultancy contracts with large firms offer a more interesting and more profitable business than seeking to secure in-house design contracts, but discovers that the chief design engineer is really only interested in working in the studio which he helped set up, is facing a similar situation. In both cases, the solution is either reorganize or disintegrate, because key people could have been pursuing strategies at cross-purposes to those of the owner of the business. In the absence of clearer descriptions of the duties and responsibilities of the various jobs, and a clear declaration from the owner about where the business should be heading, these differences may not have emerged, and the confusion would have become even more deep rooted. *The Barclays Guide to Managing Staff for the Small Business* describes many of these organizational issues, especially how to produce an accurate job description, in much greater detail.

Overcrowding

The other main growth problem that is directly related to the people who work in your business is the question of overcrowding. The problem may become apparent as your staff begin to complain about having to share their offices with too many people, or if somebody points out that the boxes of supplies in the corridor are a safety hazard. Another set of complaints, which are also related to the problem of confusion discussed in the previous section, is that telephones remain unanswered, messages do not get passed or picked up, and it is often very difficult to get an outside line to call an important customer. Perhaps many of these complaints can be silenced by installing a more modern telephone exchange, but usually they are yet another sign of overcrowding. If you have your own office, you may not be fully aware of the problem, but should you decide that you need extra staff then you will realize that you have nowhere to put them.

However, it is not so simple to conjure space out of nowhere or even to find exactly ideal premises. Indeed, moving or building extensions can be rather costly and is always extremely disruptive. Therefore, before even thinking about moving or getting in the builders, you should start by analysing exactly why you are running out of space. How you go about analysing your premises needs and how you choose the best strategy from several complex options are dealt with in chapter 5. For the present, it is important to determine whether you have a lack of space, an inefficient use of space, or an excess of unnecessary objects, equipment or staff. If you have been steadily growing without loss of profits and you have been increasing certain types of staff whenever the increase in orders reaches certain levels, then you probably do face a genuine problem of overcrowding.

On the other hand, if you have been taking on staff because you have been increasing your range of activities, and if your growth has been accompanied by a drop in profits, then you have a problem of uncontrolled growth. In these circumstances, the marketing analysis discussed in chapter 7 and the financial control techniques outlined in chapter 6 should help you to identify the unprofitable or loss-making parts of your business and reduce them or close them entirely. Of course, to be able to realize that your spread of activities is too broad or that one particular area of your business is punching a hole in your profits requires your having enough time for planning and analysis, which may be a big problem in itself. In terms of overcrowding, however, careful pruning should cut back your un-kempt undergrowth and judicious weeding should leave your business rosier and relieve your problem without the expense of a disruptive relocation or refurbishment.

For instance, if the engineering example mentioned in the previous section – Batchjob – found that they needed a new machine for every jobbing contract, it would be a race between running out of money and running out of space. Similarly, if the rates offered by the computer bureau example – Compburo – for contract word-processing were too low, it would not be long before word-processing orders began to crowd out more profitable and less space-consuming consultancy contracts.

Question 3   Do you suspect that any areas of your business may be unprofitable or using up more than a fair share of labour or space?

Before deciding that any area of your business is not pulling its weight or that it has more staff or space than it needs, you should make sure that you are using your existing space efficiently. Again, this is covered in more detail in chapter 5, but there are a few simple checks that you can try. If you measure how much usable space there is in each room and divide by the number of people in the room, you can quickly identify which rooms are overcrowded and which are under-utilized. Short-term relief may lie in achieving a better occupancy balance between the rooms, in changing the location of activities to more appropriate rooms or even in freeing some of the non-usable space by adopting more efficient methods of storage. In the longer term, however, if you are growing fairly steadily you will need a longer-lasting solution which gives you more average usable space per employee than you currently have.

Low staff morale

As the problems of unplanned growth begin to make their presence felt, it is extemely likely that your staff will be adversely affected. Overcrowding, confusion, no time to think or take stock and the other problems of growth could make your business a fairly unpleasant place to work in. Add to this the uncertainty that is caused by unplanned growth, and you have a recipe for creating high staff turnover and high absenteeism. Once again, however, if you are suffering from such a problem, you should make sure that the high loss of staff is not due to other causes. Obviously, if your industry or the region where you conduct your business is prone to high staff turnover or absenteeism, then your problems in this area may not be due to uncontrolled growth. Also, uncontrolled growth cannot be blamed if you are paying your employees below the going rates for your type of business in your region.

Question 4   In general, do you find it difficult to find the staff you need and, recently, have you been losing staff at a faster rate than normal?

To some extent, the problem of finding suitably skilled or motivated staff is a difficulty faced by most small businesses that have to compete in the labour market with bigger businesses. However, if staff have been leaving at a faster rate than normal it may pay you to check that your pay and conditions have not fallen below those of other, nearby firms in similar businesses to yours. Whatever the cause, this type of staff problem is not good for the health of your business. If you are satisfied that your pay and conditions are reasonable, the clue to overcoming the problem lies, once again, in clarifying the lines of responsibility and in making sure that all employees understand what they should be doing. Next, you need to work on motivating your staff. This will be discussed in more detail in chapter 4, but one sound piece of advice which holds true in most situations is to make sure that you take the trouble to praise good performance. If you are entering a period of growth, you need to take your workforce with you. Their enthusiasm, goodwill and identification with your business may be your only defence against some of the more acute problems of growth.

Weak financial records and cash management

It is a common refrain among accountants and bankers that small businesses (whether or not they are growing) leave a lot to be desired in the way they keep their financial records. If you feel that you are weak in this department, unplanned growth will bring its own extra chaos into your present accounting systems. You need to keep clear records of your sales, your purchases, your payouts, any credit that you have given and any loans or credit that you have taken out, and have a clear idea of when the various sums of money should be coming in or going out. All these matters are covered extensively in *The Barclays Guide to Financial Management for the Small Business*, which also highlights many of the dangers that spring from poor record-keeping. Indeed, the most common causes of business failure include *overtrading* and poor debtor control – both of which spring from a lack of accurate records.

In fact, overtrading is very much directly connected to the process of growth and is covered in more detail in chapter 7. Basically, overtrading refers to the situation that many fast-growing small businesses find themselves in when they begin to run out of cash, despite a full or expanding order book. As you grow, both your payments and your revenue also grow, but overtrading occurs when you are paying your outgoings faster than you are collecting your incomings. Sometimes, severe problems can occur because all or part of your business is inherently unprofitable. Frequently, however, the business is quite profitable but there is an unacceptable delay in collecting due payments. Obviously, this is also connected to your debtor-control system and, if you end up suffering from too many bad debts, to your credit-control system. All these systems and all antidotes to overtrading depend, in the first instance, on keeping regular and accurate financial records.

An increase in workload without any increase in income or profits is the classic sign of overtrading and a common sign that your growth is out of control. Stated as simply as this it seems obvious, but the catch with overtrading is that your business can actually be making reasonable profits on paper but the cash is not coming in when you absolutely need it. However, without reasonably accurate and up-to-date records, you will not know even the basic fact of whether your business is currently profitable or not. The need to identify the profitable parts of your business has already been mentioned on p. 4 and assumes even greater importance in this case.

Question 5 Have you begun to have problems in making sure that the cash you are owed is coming in on time? Have you been embarrassed recently over not having the cash available to make necessary payments?

If your business is fairly busy and you have experienced either or both of these problems lately, then it is likely that you are overtrading. Of course, it is worse if the new orders are not profitable. It is not uncommon in new firms to accept every order that is offered and to forget to take into account the costs or resources required to complete each new contract. When the real or unsuspected extra costs – such as increases in staff, equipment and supplies – are taken into account, an apparently profitable job can switch quickly into a loss. If the full costs have not been taken into account, the job will entail extra, unexpected work (hence lack of time, confusion and reduced staff morale) and reduced or negative profit, which means too much work and too little pay (for yourself and your employees). Obviously, operating at a loss is not a wise strategy for any firm, especially for a small firm that is growing. If growth is producing an increasing hole in your finances, you need to correct it before you disappear.

Summary

This chapter has examined the common problems associated with unplanned growth – lack of time, organizational confusion, overcrowding, low morale and overtrading. Each section contained hints about some of the methods that can be used effectively in overcoming these problems. These hints, and other less obvious strategies, will be expanded upon in subsequent chapters. However, each problem is potentially serious enough to bring down your business if left untreated, so it may pay you to complete the following chapter which aims at helping you to analyse exactly where your main growth problem lies. Finally, if you gave affirmative answers to several questions in Exhibit 1.1, you should start thinking immediately about what you might have to do about the problems that you feel currently threaten your business. The rest of this book is devoted to providing you with the means for finding your own solutions.

Key points

- Find time to plan your growth.
- Avoid confusion by making sure that everyone knows their own duties and responsibilities.
- Try not to cram too many people, records or pieces of equipment into limited space.
- Boost morale by involving everyone in your plans for growth.
- Make sure that your growth is generating sufficient revenue to cover the increased costs.

2

Identifying your own main growing pains

Outline

Not all expanding businesses suffer from all the problems of growth at once or even at all. Indeed, growth will affect each business in its own particular way, although it is safe to say that the businesses that fail to plan will suffer more problems, more acutely. To help you diagnose your own business growth problems, we look at:

- the importance of setting attainable, relevant goals
- the structure and flexibility of your organization
- the demands of growing markets on your business
- the need for organizational and financial controls
- accommodating the physical and psychological effects of growth

---

It is helpful to be able to describe your main growing problems accurately, but accurate descriptions are not enough. You need to be able to identify the root causes of the particular problems which have been afflicting your own business. Because the problems of growth are closely related, your apparent main problem may actually be a symptom of a more underlying weakness and, as with health, it is better to cure the cause than merely to relieve the symptoms. The aim of this chapter is to help you analyse the fundamental problems – workforce, marketing, financial, motivational, premises – in your business that have led to its unpredictable growth and to suggest strategies for getting your business back on track. Apart from identifying your fundamental business growth problems – each of which will be dealt with in more detail in subsequent chapters – the aim of this chapter is also to identify basic good practice in each of these important areas.

Setting attainable goals

The effects of unplanned growth do not only affect your business performance. There are also personal effects that have to be managed. Of course, it is outside the scope of this book to analyse in any depth how you spend your leisure or what balance you should maintain between your business and your family life. Nevertheless, it is worth noting that growth can lead to overwork and that an excessive devotion to work – apart from its effects on your health and social life – usually results in inefficiencies and an unbalanced approach at work. Certainly, any business manager who is serious about learning about market response and changes in customer tastes (see chapter 7, pp. 104–123) cannot afford to remain permanently closed up at work surrounded only by business problems.

The effects of unplanned growth on your own business performance can distort your perceptions and judgement, leading you to set inappropriate priorities, adopt short-term responses rather than longer-term solutions and become over-sentimental about products that have come to the end of their life cycles (see chapter 7). Paradoxically, the strains of growth can also lead you to increase your own workload and resist sharing work with other people, even though growing businesses need managers who spend increasingly more time on planning than on daily, routine activities.

By now, it should be clear that your business goals and how you communicate them to your staff have a powerful influence on most aspects of your business and lie at the heart of managing the growth process. All good management – in whatever sized business – rests on the fundamental principle that the manager is able to identify longer-term goals and the shorter-term and immediate objectives which will ultimately lead to those goals. For instance, a business owner who ultimately wants the business to develop into an international conglomerate will have different goals and expectations from an owner who only wants the business to provide a reasonable living. Similarly, a manager who strives for a larger market share will be more concerned about sales and less about profits than one who wants to earn a reputation for high quality or than one who aims at achieving a high rate of return on invested capital.

The second important point is that the goals and objectives cannot be set in concrete for all time. Indeed, one year can be close to eternity for some businesses. The fact that you are facing problems connected with business growth is a clear demonstration that businesses – and certainly your business – do not stand still. Indeed, even if you wanted your business to remain in a stable, unchanging state, outside forces would soon knock you off balance. You only have to look outside at the national balance of payments, changing patterns of trade, fluctuating interest rates, unstable inflation and, just over the horizon, the Single European Market, to realize that the business environment is as changeable as the weather. Consequently, your business aims and objectives cannot be rigid but must be sufficiently adaptable to prevailing conditions while retaining the essence of your principal reason for being in business.

Question 6 What are your own longer-term goals for your business?

Basically, you have to ask yourself why you are in business and you have to try to be as objective, as honest and as direct with yourself as you can be. For instance, do any of the common reasons mentioned above – growth, profits, larger market share, producing quality products, providing a reasonable living – apply to you? Are you in business to make money or because you want to be independent and work for yourself? Or is it more the case that you cannot find another job that you really like, or because you want to create something? There are many other reasons and yours may be unique. It is most important that you are consistent and clear about your main business goals and that you make sure that your business reflects them. Examples of the dangers of having conflicting business goals inside the same organization were discussed on pp. 6–8 of the previous chapter.

Once you have identified your own main business goals, you then have to decide whether it is really practical and attainable, or whether it is destined to remain a vision of an ideal future. In the event that you are having a disagreement with other key people in your business, it will pay you to cast a critical eye over your own business goals to see if they really stand up to scrutiny. For instance, in the examples mentioned above – Batchjob and Compburo – it may be that the owners' personal goals could only be attained after expertise and capital had been built up by, respectively, taking on longer-term orders for set components and by using the studio to produce designs for external clients. In other words, the preferences of the technical staff may have been better intermediate goals for the business, even though the owners' longer-term views would ultimately prevail.

However, it should be stressed that it is very difficult for most businesses to identify precisely the most appropriate shorter-term, intermediate and longer-term goals at any given time. It is always easier to see in retrospect what your goals should have been because it is almost impossible to find up-to-the-minute information. Also, sometimes it is only possible to get the right perspective on events after you have had time to consider some of the consequences and side-effects. Even extensive business experience may not shield you from getting it wrong.

The key to small-business leadership lies in selecting appropriate goals. Which goals you decide are important will depend on the nature of your business, your personal ambitions and the immediate problems which you face. Of course, it would be a mistake to try to do everything at once, and you must work out your own set of priorities but, in general, there are two crucial points to consider in goal selection:

- the goals must produce evident benefits
- the goals must be attainable

For you to inspire a highly motivated performance in other people, you have to be able to demonstrate to them that your proposed outcome is desirable and that their efforts are capable of producing that desirable outcome. People will not produce their peak performance if they believe that their efforts are a waste of time. Also, you must make sure that each goal is not too general. Indeed, it must be capable of being broken down into more precise steps and tasks which – if satisfactorily completed – will lead to success. For instance, 'increasing profits' is a general aim but 'increasing the sales of our most profitable product or service' is a goal which requires you to decide on the size of proposed increase, the likely time span and the preferred strategy – each one of which generates a series of sub-goals and tasks to be completed. Therefore, the notion that the goal must be worthwhile and attainable may be further refined to:

- the goal must actually benefit the business
- the goal must be seen to benefit the business
- the goal must suggest the operations necessary for its attainment
- the business must have the resources to attain the goal
- the business must have the collective will to attain the goal

The ability to set realistic goals and communicate them to the other people in your business is basic to your leading your business rather than having it lead you. Setting clear goals is the first step in the development of your own growth strategy and is essential if you are to organize your business effectively.

Organizing for growth

Apart from an obvious increase in confusion at work, the organizational demands that growth puts on your business are usually experienced as either a lack of resources or a lack of suitable staff. Certainly, as you expand your output – whether your products are goods or services – you will also increase your consumption of the resources (machines, material inputs, energy, information, people and so on) that enable you to produce your products. If the expansion continues, you will eventually have to take some very important investment and organizational decisions. Indeed, you may have already reached the point where you are considering acquiring new machines or more staff. The business implications in stepping up your costs in this way are covered in *The Barclays Guide to Financial Management for the Small Business*. The organizational implications usually fall into two broad areas, depending on whether you have been using your existing resources efficiently and to their full capacity, or whether you need to create a structure to get the best use out of your new resources.

Of course, each business requires its own unique mix of resources but, in the final analysis, all firms need suitably skilled staff to utilize their resources efficiently. Therefore, the main organizational problems can usually be dealt with as people problems. The five points of realistic goal selection in a smaller business, covered in the previous section, already hint at the need for you to carry your workforce with you in tackling the adverse effects of rapid unplanned business expansion. Up till now, we have mainly considered the business impact of unplanned growth on your firm and some of the personal effects on you. However, it should be clear that unplanned growth will have considerable effects on your workforce. Even more to the point, the steps that you take to overcome the worst effects of unplanned growth will also impact on your workforce. Sometimes, a quiet haven amid chaos seems immediately preferable to accepting the need to change and confront the chaos head on.

When workloads and throughputs in rapidly growing businesses rise dramatically, it is not uncommon to find that some of the staff retreat into the security of their own job, evading responsibility and even adding their gloomy observations or predictions to an already confused and demoralized situation. Even if your business is not growing quite so dramatically, you can probably identify similar personalities in your own firm. If growth has also meant the taking on of new, inexperienced staff, the confusion will do little to help them learn their new skills or deal with the stress of starting a new job. Indeed, their lack of experience will itself contribute to the confusion and, if nobody can spare the time to train or advise them, their confusion and the firm's growth problems will only be compounded.

Of course, this picture of chaos seems particularly dire in a business that is expanding rapidly without any real structure. Nevertheless, even if your business is growing at a slower rate with much less evident chaos, it is highly likely that the same processes are at work. You are likely to find that most of the difficulties that you are experiencing with your own form of unplanned growth involve you in coming to terms with the organizational issues confronting your business. For instance, many very small firms, and even some firms with up to a dozen employees (especially if many of the workers are engaged in similar, routine tasks), owe much of their initial success to the personal and direct style of management of their owners. In growing businesses, however, a strongly personal style can become over-centralized if the owner does not find a way of letting other people share the workload and take certain decisions. In the absence of some kind of structure and agreed allocation of tasks, albeit on an informal basis, the upsurge in decisions and work that accompanies expansion can swamp an over-involved owner-manager, leaving the business with nobody to handle the overflow.

Too much central control stifles the flexibility and staff dedication that are the hallmark of really successful smaller independent businesses. In all sizes of business, the people who work in the business take their cue from the people at the top. If you insist on being involved in every decision, and feel that you need to be informed of everything that happens in your business, then it is unlikely that many of your employees or junior partners will have a very clear idea of where their responsibilities and duties start and finish. Even worse, if they do manage to secure their own area of responsibility, they are likely to be very wary and jealous of letting anyone else encroach upon it. In their more limited way, your subordinates are likely to be even less open with other people in the business than you are. Even though they and especially you may be very hard-working, the ethos of hard work may not be enough to enthuse the other employees, if they feel excluded.

Going to the other extreme, however, if you are fairly lax and rather 'laid back', then – although morale may be high – there will be no structure and no sense that quality, delivery deadlines or goals matter. Indeed, an over-relaxed regime is not likely to notice when jobs do not get completed or when orders are not delivered. The lack of responsibility will eventually lead to the disintegration of the business. In a very small business all of these problems are containable, and the close direct contact between the people who work in the business substitutes for more effective (and, ultimately, more flexible) systems of communication. Whether your business tends to one extreme or to the other you will know, but, even if you feel you are in the middle, you may still have severe organizational and internal communications problems.

Question 7   Do you feel that your natural management style is too centralized or too lax (or fluctuates from one to the other)? Do you feel that the people in your business have problems defining their areas of responsibility?

Many of the issues connected with finding answers to these questions are covered in the next two chapters. For the moment it is important for you to think about whether your business is presently organized in a way that will help you achieve your business goals (those that you identified in question 6, p. 16). Think about the main tasks that have to be completed for you to know that your customers are satisfied. In particular, try to identify the functions within your business that are necessary for its survival and growth and identify the people, apart from yourself, who ensure that each function of your business performs satisfactorily.

For instance, production, administration, storage and distribution will be important functions in most small engineering firms and the respective key people – depending on the size of the business – will be the production manager or supervisor, the secretary or office manager, the storeman, the despatch clerk or the delivery manager. If the firm manufactures consumer products or is keen to expand, then it is likely also to have someone attending to the sales and/or marketing function. Retailing, wholesaling and various services also need to have people involved on different aspects of sales and marketing (and often someone handling purchasing as well). Indeed, in most smaller firms the owner takes on the sales and marketing function personally – frequently without learning the technical skills involved (if this applies to you, look at *The Barclays Guide to Marketing for the Small Business*).

The main point is that, while each business has its own mix of functions and people who perform them, often the matching of functions to people just evolves without much planning. This is particularly true of growing businesses which often do not even have the time to think about how they are organized. Exhibit 2.1, showing the two fictional firms mentioned earlier – the small engineers

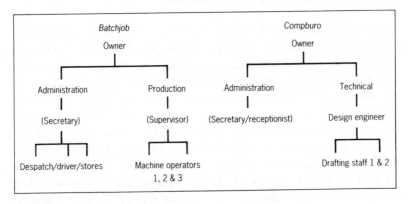

Exhibit 2.1 Organizational charts of Batchjob and Compburo

Batchjob and the computer-design bureau Compburo – can serve to illustrate the point. There is a slight conflict between Batchjob's ambitious owner and the more cautious production supervisor. At the moment the balance favours the supervisor because Batchjob is working within its technical organizational capacity (the supervisor could easily handle three or four more similar machines and several more machine and lathe operators) but the responsibility for finding more stand-alone contracts rests only with the owner.

If Batchjob's owner is sure that the future lies in gaining several small independent contracts to escape from the dependency of sub-contracting low-value components, then he will have to expand the Administration to include someone to help with sales and marketing as well as keep an eye on the costs and organizational implications for Production. Similarly, Compburo's owner is faced with either training one of the existing drafting staff or finding and appointing a better qualified person to work independently in client companies. Of course, this decision would have profound organizational implications not only with the existing design engineer but also in terms of control. This important area of management is covered in chapter 4 but, in the meantime, try to draw a diagram that best describes the way your business is currently organized and list the advantages and disadvantages that your current business structure has in relation to the attainment of your business goals.

The demands of a growth market

Having considered your business goals and the more fundamental aspects of your business organization, the third factor to consider is precisely where your business fits into its main market. Once again, most of the issues relating to your products and their markets are extensively analysed in *The Barclays Guide to Marketing for the Small Business*. However, even at a more general level, it is important to examine how the effects of growth relate to your main market, because you could easily slip off the growth curve if you do not fully understand where your business stands. Exhibit 2.2 illustrates the crisis points that smaller growing businesses have to pass if they are to grow successfully, and you can see where your business currently stands and where you would like it to be in the future.

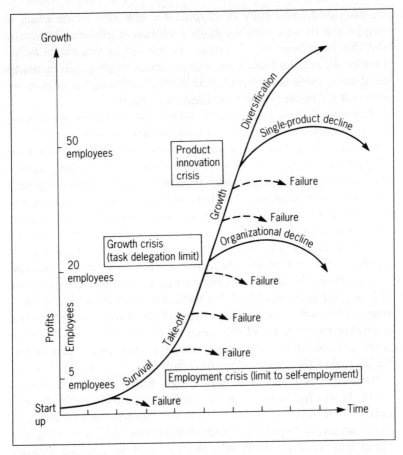

Exhibit 2.2 Growth crisis points on the small expanding business growth curve
Source: adapted from C. Gray and P. Burns, *Managing the Growing Business*. (The Small Business Programme, Open University, 1990).

The first crisis point is that of survival. More than half the number of new firms do not manage to overcome their first major crisis point to make it beyond the survival stage into the growth stage. The next crisis faced by many new or very small businesses is when they realize that they have to employ at least one other person apart from members of the family. Indeed, deciding whether to employ someone else and ensuring that you get the right person are probably still problems for you if your growth has been fairly recent (these issues are discussed more fully in chapter 4). The next major crisis is simply how to cope with the many problems of unplanned growth, and this large issue is, of course, the subject of this entire book. Finally, for smaller businesses that are about to grow into medium-sized ones, there is the problem of diversification and how to move into being a multi-product business (see chapter 7).

Any one of these crisis points can be enough to sink most small firms, even those that seem to have no trouble growing. This is partly due to a host of financial, marketing and organizational problems, but also partly due to many businesses not fully under-standing why they are growing. Basically, there are two dangerous areas of potential ignorance. First, your firm could be growing not because of any special quality it possesses but because your products are selling in an expanding market. A rapidly growing market has its own dynamic, which quickly becomes apparent to businesses in similar fields and to entrepreneurs on the lookout for business opportunities. If you are not fully aware of why your products are selling (and that there may be increasing opportunities for new, related products), you could find yourself in at the ground floor but overtaken by faster-rising, newer entrants to the market. On a large scale, the fate of Britain's motor industry (cars, lorries and motor-bikes) makes this point rather forcefully.

Secondly, you may have unwittingly found a valuable market niche. If you fail to focus on the products that meet the wants and needs of this segment of the market, you run the risk of dissipating your energies and spreading yourself too thinly. Without a clear idea about why your products sell, you can end up ignoring genuine customers while fruitlessly trying to satisfy phantom customers in the wider market. Take, for example, our fictional computer-designing services firm, Compburo. If they found that their attempts to offer their computer-designing skills on-site to their clients were very successful but did not realize that that was because of a widespread shortage of skilled staff and not because clients felt Compburo designers were inherently better than other designers, they could easily fail to see that they were offering a very specialized service even within the technological field of computing services. Insisting on battling with other, similar firms in tendering for contracts to be completed in their own studio would be to miss the point of what makes them unique. Instead, to exploit the market niche, Compburo should transform themselves into something resembling a freelance agency for high-technology experts or else recruit more of their own computer designers to work always outside the Compburo studio.

If you are unaware of the true nature of either of these situations, you could easily start off down the wrong track as you grapple with the problems of reasserting control over your business. Obviously, if you stumble into a profitable niche in the market without being aware of it, you will not be able to exploit your market position to its fullest extent. Indeed, if the niche represents a temporary or fashionable demand, you may end up over-committed in terms of investments and stock without fully understanding why your period of uncontrolled growth has come to an end. Similarly, if you happen to be selling to a market that is expanding for reasons that are unknown to you and completely external to your firm, you will not be in a position to detect market saturation or the entry of stronger competitors. Many markets – and not only the obviously seasonal ones such as tourism, agriculture or construction – move in cycles, and it could be disastrous for your business if you are heavily investing for future growth after your market has peaked. Equally, you could be missing a tremendous opportunity if you are seriously under-capitalized at the start of a boom. In other words, to control growth and plan future strategy, you need to be aware of market trends.

Question 8   Can you describe the market for your best-selling product in terms of segments? Do you have a reasonable idea of the future prospects for the main segments: are they likely to grow, are there similar segments to which your products could appeal, or are your market segments essentially limited?

If you rely largely on one basic product, your answers to these questions should highlight one major danger that growth holds for your business. Single-product businesses are tied to the life cycle of their product and are extremely vulnerable should more efficient newcomers be attracted to their growing market. To avoid being wrecked by cyclical trends in your main market or by a decline in demand for your only product, your plans for growth must include the development of new products or new markets. This is obviously an important aspect of expansion to discuss and it will be examined in greater detail in chapter 7. Of equal importance is the need to maintain or reassert financial control over your business as it grows.

Controlling the process of growth

Even if you do have clear business goals, a flexible organizational structure and a reasonable idea of the main segments and likely future trends in your markets, you still have to have technical business skills, so that you can actually control growth through controlling your cash flow and your business costs. The main issues associated with the financial side of growth are examined in more detail in chapter 6 but, before you even start to think about introducing or improving a system of financial controls, you must make sure that your financial records have not fallen victim to unplanned growth. Every management system depends on having access to well-kept records, but one of the main symptoms of unplanned growth is sloppy or tardy record-keeping. Failure to keep accurate records produces a vicious circle in that it is often one of the effects of expansion – increasingly less time to deal with increasingly more information – yet, in turn, the lack of accurate records prevents any real planning.

In fact, how to record and use financial information is covered in *The Barclays Guide to Financial Management for the Small Business* and how to make use of staff records is covered in *The Barclays Guide to Managing Staff for the Small Business*. Also, the importance of central office and administrative functions to the structure of a growing business is discussed more fully in chapter 4. For the moment, however, if you have started your business or started to grow fairly recently, it may be helpful to highlight the basic records that most well-run smaller businesses use for controlling their costs, cash flow, profits and overall performance. First, you need to know what and when you have bought and sold goods or services. As you may need this fundamental information for a number of different purposes, it makes sense to keep separate, reasonably detailed, daily records of your sales and purchases including any VAT (usually in a *sales day book* and a *purchases day book* but maybe directly in a computer if you have the expertise).

Secondly, you should keep separate records for each of your

account customers and each of your suppliers. Each account customer should be recorded on a separate page in a *sales ledger* with information about the customer's address, phone number, banking branch, the terms of trade and any credit limits. It is common to note the date and details of each sale down the left-hand side of the page and of each payment down the right-hand side of the page. Similarly, you should keep records of your suppliers and creditors in a *purchase ledger*, again with details of your outgoing payments on the left-hand side and details of purchases on the right-hand side. Finally, you should also keep a daily record of your cash transactions – whether by credit card, cheque or cash – in a *cash book.*

If you are finding it harder to collect your payments in reasonable time, or if you have actually had to approach your bank manager in a hurry because you suddenly realized that you did not actually have enough cash in your account to cover necessary purchases or payments, then either you have not been keeping up-to-date records or you have not been using them to keep track of how your business is performing. If you suspect that your costs have risen faster than your growth in sales, or that you are paying out faster than your revenue is coming in, the confirmation – or otherwise – of your suspicions should lie in your current records if they are up-to-date. Keeping one eye on your cash balances and another on how fast your debtors are paying is extremely important for growing businesses, because one of the most common causes of failure in growing businesses is poor control of cash flow. This issue is looked at more closely in chapter 6 and fully explained in *The Barclays Guide to Financial Management for the Small Business*, and for the moment it is sufficient to point out that if your cash comes in at a slower rate than it goes out, then the problem will become more dangerous as the scale of your transactions grows.

Finally, if you have got a plan or a budget for the year, you need to know whether you are on track and, once again, the answer lies in your financial records. When your business starts growing, it is imperative that you monitor the process of growth so that you can take early corrective action. To be able to monitor the effects of growth on your business you will need to have first produced a budget of proposed expenditure and income so that you have a yardstick against which to measure any movements. Obviously, to produce such a budget and to continue to monitor any changes, you will need to keep fairly accurate and accessible financial records. It is important to avoid getting caught in an all-too-common growth trap, whereby you risk going out of business because you fail to manage your cash flow, yet you find it very hard to control your cash flow because your growth is out of control.

Just about any expanding business will experience an increase in costs as sales begin to climb. To ensure that your business survives if you are in that situation, you have to make sure that your income from sales is climbing even faster than costs, and that you are actually collecting that income within the time periods stipulated in your terms of sale. (If you do not have fairly standard terms of sale, you must make sure that your customers understand your special conditions, because, if you plan according to your terms and conditions but they pay according to custom, this could be one reason why your business growth is not running as smoothly as you would like.) If you cannot keep certain production costs down or collect your payments in time, each new sale could actually take out more cash than it brings in, and it will not be long before you overtrade your way out of cash.

Question 9   Are cash shortages one of your main business-growth problems? Are you happy about how fast your main customers pay you?

Expansion puts increased pressure on your finances, particularly because revenues from sales usually take a lot longer to come in than the costs of your rising sales take to go out. Even if your systems are reasonably efficient and your business is well organized, sudden or unexpected growth can catch you unawares, unless you monitor your regular records against your budgeted expenditure and your original expectations (in terms of costs and collection of debts).

Accommodating growth

Of course, if you are growing, or if you have reached a crucial stage in the development of your business, the first signs that you notice may be the physical effects of growth. You may suddenly realize that your present premises have become inadequate. It is worth noting, however, that the physical feeling of constriction brought about by unplanned growth may be due not only to a growing lack of space but also to your own attitudes towards growth or towards your business. On the more tangible side, it was mentioned that the physical lack of space may be due to an increase in your workforce, limitations to your storage areas for your stocks of raw materials and finished products, or design problems which are only revealed as you expand. These issues were discussed in chapter 1 (pp. 8–10) and are covered in full in chapter 5.

Basically, if you realize that you are blocked from expanding because your premises lack sufficient space, or if you feel that you need to move to establish a better image or to be more accessible to your market, you will have to start planning to move. Whether you decide to expand your existing premises or to move partially or completely are issues dealt with in chapter 5, as is the question of whether to purchase or rent. The main business point to be aware of at this stage is that the move will entail costs and that your final premises costs (insurance, maintenance, rates, services) may well be higher than your present ones. If the move has been occasioned by the need to take on more staff or more machinery, then all these costs will have to be taken into account when you decide whether the move is profitable and whether your new volumes of sales earn you as much revenue or profit as before.

Less tangibly, the issues of your own motivation and your business image also have to be considered, not only on a personal level but also as part of your business objectives. Indeed, if you have a clear idea about your own business motivation and the image that you want for your firm, this indicates that your growth has not been entirely unplanned, because you have definite goals. On other levels, however, the implications are less rosy. For instance, you must be sure that your goals are attainable in the time scale that you have set for them. If you move to a more prestigious address, not because it helps your business but just because you like the area, then you are saddling your business with unnecessary overheads. Similarly, if you want to treble your sales by next year, it would not be wise to rush into much larger premises until there are some signs that your sales are actually going up and some indication that continued sales are likely.

On a different level, it may be that you do not wish to move or that any feasible move would take you too far away. Even more importantly, you may feel that your unanticipated growth has disturbed a life style that you prefer to maintain at its present level. If you would prefer to stay where you are but your sales have reached a critical level where you need more staff, then you have to control your growth without moving. The first area to examine is your current staffing. You need to be sure that your present operation really is working close to full capacity. If you feel that everybody is fully stretched, the next area to examine is your storage. It may be that you are storing too much stock or, even worse, storing old products which you were unable to sell. Either way, you should address the issues of stock control. Indeed, this will become more important as you grow so you should examine your stock control system even if you intend to move or to expand.

Question 10   If you feel that you have grown too big for your present premises, how do you feel about moving? Do you want to grow much beyond your present size?

If you are not too sure that you actually want to get much bigger, you should examine some of the areas mentioned above with the aim of improving the efficiency of your operation without increasing its size. You could also consider raising your prices to ration your volume of sales. The net result should be a lower workload with higher income and profits. Another area to consider if you do not want to grow out of your present premises is the use of computers. While it is a myth that computers will create the 'paperless' office, computers can handle repetitive tasks and are very valuable for dealing with accounts. Also, word-processing packages can make life a lot easier and are quicker for typists and secretaries. If currently you find that routine operations are taking up a lot of space, then a computer may actually save you space (although it is mainly time that they save – once you have learned how to use them). The use of computers in business is covered in *The Barclays Guide to Computing for the Small Business*. Finally, if the increased volume of sales is pushing you out of your present premises, you can always consider splitting your premises by retaining your administration on your most presentable site and moving storage and fabrication to a cheaper one.

Summary

In this chapter, the broad responses to your own particular problems of unplanned growth were outlined. More detailed analysis and strategies for dealing with growth problems are suggested in the following chapters. The issues and problems discussed in this chapter, however, should help you to identify any staffing or skills resources that you may need. These will be considered in chapter 4.

Key points

- Set goals that are both relevant to your business objectives and attainable.
- Make sure that your medium-term objectives can be split into separate, easily understood steps.
- Organize your business so that it has a recognizable structure yet remains flexible in the face of change.
- Take the trouble to identify and understand your main markets and customer segments, especially those that are generating your growth.
- Constantly monitor a few key, appropriate performance and financial variables so that you are not caught out by sudden surprises.
- Make sure that the effects of growth are not pushing you in a direction you want to avoid, or into costly premature decisions about equipment, premises or staff.

3

Finding time to plan

Outline

The key to controlling the problems of unexpected growth lies in planning, but most smaller businesses find it difficult to allocate sufficient time or importance to planning. It is extremely important, therefore, to make sure that you find the time to plan where your business is heading. To do this effectively you need to be able to:

- manage time effectively
- organize your work efficiently
- communicate and use information effectively
- develop suitable management systems

Clearly, if you are suffering the effects of unplanned growth, then at least part of the solution must lie in introducing some form of planning into your business. However, it is much easier to talk about planning than it is actually to get down to producing a plan for your business or even planning a relatively simple business task. One of the reasons is that in most small businesses, especially those suffering from unplanned growth, there never seems to be any spare time. The aim of this chapter is to help you develop techniques for managing your own use of time, then to suggest systems for cutting time wastage in your business. Finally, the aim is to help you use the freed time for effective planning – which also means outlining practical methods for effective planning.

Identifying your main time wasters

Whatever combination of time wasters that you identified in chapter 1 (p. 5) as your personal bugbears, it is important to realize that your growing business actually demands more of your time for planning and making decisions. Therefore, every needless interruption and every minute that you spend on a low-priority task is robbing your business of its most valuable asset – the time that you have to spend on planning your future business objectives and strategy. Because your time is so precious, you need to be ruthless with the time wasters – telephone calls, late appointments, unfocused meetings, social chit-chat in the middle of the day, involvement in relatively unimportant problems, and dozens of other time bandits.

Indeed, on top of these time management problems which are common to many businesses, managers of growing small businesses frequently face another major time waster. There is a pronounced tendency for the founder or founders of small businesses to attempt to do too many overlapping jobs – especially lower-priority, routine or inappropriate jobs. If you have a new business or have recently started up, it is not too hard to understand how this particular growth inefficiency develops. If you started business as a self-employed sole-trader, you had no choice but to do everything yourself. Even a small partnership or small business employing a couple of people has to be flexible to survive, and everybody is expected to be able to chip in and turn their hand to most sides of the business. Indeed, you may never have started growing unless you were flexible in this way.

However, as you begin to be more sure of the survival of your business and as you begin to attract more trade, the question of your own role in the business has to be addressed. As mentioned in the previous chapter, this raises deeper questions about your own personal business goals which, in more ways than one, are the fundamental issue of this book. Whatever your ultimate business goals, however, as your business grows, there comes a point when it is no longer economically sensible for you to spend much time on certain tasks. Some of these lower-priority tasks are obvious – making tea, stuffing envelopes, answering routine enquiries. One of the first signs of growth is the realization that you need to offload certain tasks that consume your time and interfere with the tasks that are more central to how you and your business make money. Later, though it may not be so clear, you will need to delegate even the responsibility for many of these more central tasks.

The problem with growth is that it usually happens initially without any obvious side-effects and the fact that some tasks have a lower priority may only become apparent as you begin to feel pressures from the lack of time. Indeed, even then, some lower-priority tasks may seem less obvious because it is necessary that they get done properly, such as taking telephone orders or delivering completed work to customers. You may even convince yourself that they have a higher priority because you are also getting important feedback from the market or maintaining valuable customer contact. In fact, if you had more time, an analysis of your existing sales would help you achieve both these objectives much more effectively.

If you do feel that your management of time needs improvement, the solution is not too difficult to outline. The main difficulty is in making sure that you start right now and that you persist until you arrive at a method that suits your present needs and is flexible enough to accommodate your future growth.

- Break your working day into half-hour units and, recording as you go (with the help of a timer if you find it helpful), note how you spend each half-hour of your working week.
- Analyse how much time you spent on work that you consider to be fairly high-priority and productive; how much time you spent on planning; how much time on travel; how much time on low-priority tasks; and how much time you consider was wasted.
- Decide for yourself suitable methods for increasing your time spent on planning and higher-priority tasks while reducing time wasted on low-priority tasks and other things.
- Each evening or each morning, list the tasks and activities that you need to do during the following day.
- Assign priorities to each of the tasks, including the target time of day for the task completion.

Even before you have finished logging your use of time over one week, some solutions will have occurred to you. Even being aware of just how much time you feel is non-productive can have a beneficial effect on your time management, particularly if you are clear in your own mind about where you want your business to go. Remember, it is important to keep your ultimate objectives in mind as a yardstick when deciding on your higher-priority tasks.

Setting priorities

The key to efficient time management lies in deciding which tasks cannot wait, which tasks are central to your job and which undone tasks cause bottlenecks. These are the vital tasks which should have first priority. How much time you have to allocate to them will depend on how urgent the task is and on the number of competing tasks. It is worth noting that urgent tasks need not be vital (indeed, a great deal of time is often wasted in attending to urgent but non-vital tasks such as low-key telephone enquiries, unexpected visitors, other people's crises, and so on). The priority of tasks on any given day will depend on their relative importance to your business and the likely knock-on effects of leaving the task undone.

Basically, most day-to-day activities are the routine management tasks connected with keeping the business going, such as dealing with customer complaints, keeping the accounts and invoicing up to date, ensuring that deliveries do go out on time, building staff motivation, and so on. These types of activities are concerned with *maintaining* the business at its existing level and are often contrasted with *initiating* tasks, which are the more planned, innovative and strategic tasks associated with growth. The initiating tasks include taking on more staff, trying new products, updating production, introducing new technology or new procedures, and so on. There is sometimes a danger that too many initiating tasks can be disruptive, but every growing business – if it is to continue to grow yet control its growth – needs to ensure that neither type of task is ignored.

It is likely that your business will quickly go under if essential maintaining tasks are allowed to slip. The danger is even more acute if other people in your business rely on your completing a task before they can complete their own work. For instance, if all purchases have to receive your approval, or if you feel you should inspect all finished products, then a couple of days off sick or away at an important meeting will lead to idleness while you are not there and a mountain of urgent and vital tasks when you return. However, even if you delegate authority, subject to agreed budgets and objectives, your maintaining tasks will be more vital but usually less urgent – mainly those of monitoring performance or dealing with longer-term problems. It is equally clear that the business could grind to a halt or be driven out of business by its rivals if not enough initiating tasks are undertaken. Again, a constructive policy of delegation will liberate you to spend more time on initiating activities.

Overall, initiating tasks are very important for a growing business because it is flexibility and willingness to try new approaches or techniques which set a company apart from static, established firms. However, initiating tasks should not always command top priority in your working day. A business must first survive if it is to grow and survival demands that maintaining tasks are not neglected. Also, there is little point in introducing innovation for its own sake. Initiating behaviour is only helpful if it leads to the attainment of your business goals. This is equally true of maintaining behaviour and those tasks which lead to your achieving your business objectives are usually called *active* tasks.

By contrast, the routine tasks and those which normally come in response to a letter, telephone call or visit are called *reactive* tasks. It may be more helpful, therefore, to distinguish between active and reactive tasks. It is the active tasks which should increasingly occupy your day if you are using your time productively, while the reactive tasks are those that many busy managers actually spend too much time on.

You are the person best placed to decide how active or reactive you should be in your business. However, it is worth repeating the point made above. If you are interested in seeing your business grow, then you should make space for the active, initiating tasks. Typically, these are the tasks which involve planning and which force you to think about alternatives to existing practice, new ways of doing things. Unfortunately, the major problem for busy managers of growing businesses is that these important planning and innovative tasks are often those classified as vital but non-urgent. These are usually the tasks which get set aside to be 'done when there is enough time'. If you are already suffering from unplanned growth, however, there is never enough time.

Organizing the working week

As your business grows (whether it is a retailing, manufacturing or service business), your job as a planner and coordinator becomes more important. Yet, although you should be making more time for active, initiating tasks, you cannot completely ignore all the urgent short-notice tasks – especially if there is an element of crisis or if important customers are involved. This brings us back to square one – the classic 'catch 22' situation – where there are too many things to do because you have no time to plan. Yet, you have no time for taking stock of your situation and planning because there are too many things to do.

The first step out of the maze involves identifying the tasks you spent time on during the past week which were both non-vital and reactive (ignoring whether they were urgent or non-urgent). In essence, these are the unnecessary, unimportant, uncalled-for inter-ruptions which steal your time. As they are non-vital, they can be put to one side while you examine your current work-flow system. If you have doubts about delegating any of these tasks, then you still believe deep down that they are vital. Only you can decide which tasks are important for you and vital for the successful growth of your business, but it is wise to resist the temptation to take on too much responsibility, because every task has to take up some time.

The next step is to examine the tasks which were both vital and reactive – arising from the sudden or persistent crises that spring up and have to be dealt with. Urgent or non-urgent, they are vital and demand your attention. If they were maintaining tasks, the next question to address is why your present system broke down and why your presence was required to deal with the problem. What was the essential incident which was missing (or unexpectedly present) and which caused the crisis, and how frequently do such incidents occur? You should ask similar questions about previous changes that you have had to introduce. What was the critical incident which caused a new course of action or procedure to be initiated, and how frequently are these incidents likely to occur in the future? In conducting this *critical incidents analysis*, as it is called, try to avoid the temptation to lay all the blame on external causes, because the purpose of the analysis is to identify areas where you have the power to take action.

In growing businesses, however, a common source of critical incidents lies in the internal-people area. If this is true for you, you probably need to know more about recruiting more staff, training existing staff or reorganizing the way your business is run. To

37

decide precisely which solution seems to be the most sensible, you should look once again at the actual critical incidents. If, for example, you have been spending a lot of time complaining to suppliers and dealing with complaints from customers and your own production people because of wrongly specified supplies, your ordering procedures need to be improved. In terms of priorities, you have little choice but to respond to customer complaints. However, never forget that each conversation with a customer, your production people or your suppliers takes time away from the time available for dealing with other important business matters. Always make sure that these conversations help you come up with a solution for avoiding similar problems in the future.

The critical incidents analysis can point you in the right direction. If your invoices were not going out on time as well, it would appear that you need a new secretary or that the present one is overworked and that you now need to think about your office administration. Or it may mean that you need a production supervisor to ensure that not only are the orders correctly specified, but also that supplies are ordered in anticipation rather than when stocks have run out. A quick glance at the other critical incidents should give you a strong clue to the right solution.

Thus, the most urgent (reactive) problem is to deal with the aggrieved customer, but the real (initiating) management priority is to sort out the organizational problems. In this sense, it becomes clear that time management is more about management than about time. What is important from a time-management perspective is that taking action will itself involve active, initiating tasks and that you will be moving away from reactive tasks. Your relative priorities will have changed in the right direction.

Managing information flows

As your business grows and you begin to delegate responsibilities as well as tasks, you will need to maintain your overview and be in a position to monitor regularly how your whole business is performing. This may mean that you decide to hold regular meetings. If you are heading in this direction, be warned that meetings can be the greatest source of lost or wasted time and they should be avoided in most small firms unless they are absolutely necessary. However, if you feel that some meetings are necessary for you to make sure that your business functions smoothly, make sure that your meetings do serve a real purpose.

You have to decide the agenda in consultation with your key members of staff because they are more concerned with the daily, routine problems and they know which decisions really are urgent. The regular meetings should always follow much the same format and take place in a regular venue, at a time which does not interfere with the running of your business. It is a good idea that you chair the regular meetings, and that your managers chair their section meetings. It will help you keep on top of several things happening at once in your business. Also, if you are chairing, you will be able to challenge the people who hold rigid views, release information at times that suit you and decide which topics at the meeting are of more interest to your business plans. Ultimately, your system of control could well depend on the effectiveness of your meetings (Exhibit 3.1).

- Communicate the objectives of the meeting in advance
- Agree the agenda with the key participants beforehand
- Ensure that all participants have the relevant information in advance
- Protect the meeting from outside interruption
- Chair the meeting firmly by discouraging factions and interjections yet encouraging all participants to express opinions
- Cover all the points on the agenda
- Make sure that clear minutes of the meeting are produced
- Be sure that all participants are clear which issues were decided and who has responsibility for implementing the decisions

Exhibit 3.1 Guidelines for conducting effective meetings

In the real world, meetings do not always proceed as planned but these simple rules should help you make sure that your meetings are structured and useful. Remember that the success of your system of control depends on the regular meetings allowing the free flow of information, promoting coordination, ensuring proper discussion of issues and helping you and your key staff clarify your and their thinking about future plans and targets. If a proposed meeting seems unlikely to help in any of these areas, you should question seriously whether it is worth wasting so much valuable time – yours and that of other members of your staff – holding the meeting.

An effective system of delegation and monitoring will ultimately cut down on much of the time wasted as a result of unplanned growth. The extra time should be put to effective use in planning future growth. Indeed, you should be well on the way towards developing the type of flexible structure indispensible for realizing those plans. However, in escaping the chaos and disorganization which are the most obvious features of unplanned growth, it is important to avoid one of the dangers of over-planned growth. In reacting to the growing problems of sudden expansion it is very easy to over-react and develop systems of control which are too rigid. After all, one of the great advantages that successful smaller businesses enjoy over bigger firms is their flexibility. So, just as one of the first symptoms of unplanned growth is a constant chorus of complaints from your employees that nobody knows what is going on or who is doing what, then if the constant chorus starts once again, complaining about things being too tight or about the lack of personal space, pay attention. An even more powerful warning is an increase in the numbers of people leaving – especially the people who have been with you a long time.

Of course, if you have recently reorganized, then you may expect certain people to leave, but if you find yourself surprised at other people leaving, then take note. If people feel blocked or hemmed in, they vote with their feet. However, your new organizational structure must not only accommodate the needs of your staff but also effectively address such issues as office management, planning and stock control. Computers were mentioned as a possibility to consider for overcoming certain space constrictions, and you should not ignore the possibility that a computerized system may help answer many of your planning and organizational problems. Certainly, computer-management packages designed for smaller businesses can usually help with book-keeping, cash-flow projections, profit and loss projections, word-processing, stock control and debtor control. The potential that computers have for saving you time on routine tasks is enormous. However, be warned. Before you start saving time with computers, you first of all have to invest a lot of time in learning how to use the system properly. Also, computers need maintenance and, as already mentioned, the 'paperless office' is something of a myth. Nevertheless, the extra skills that computers offer in enhancing your promotions and marketing activities and in offering swift access to data make them extremely attractive to certain types of business. Most of these issues are discussed in detail in *The Barclays Guide to Computing for the Small Business*.

Summary

In this chapter, the main problem facing all busy firms – namely, how to manage time effectively – was tackled. Because the management of time is so fundamental to the effective management of growth, the techniques of time management – identifying objectives, setting clear priorities, avoiding unnecessary interruptions, developing a systematic approach to business – lie at the heart of your strategy for developing a more structured approach to your business.

Key points

- Identify your main time wasters.
- Set clear priorities.
- Organize your work according to those priorities.
- Avoid interruptions, particularly telephone calls and informal 'chats'.
- Communicate simply and clearly with customers and colleagues.
- Start delegating your own lower-priority and time-consuming tasks to other people.
- Develop a system of task allocations appropriate for your business.

4

Developing the right team for growth

Outline

Ultimately, most business growth depends on people – the skills they have, the hours they work and the effort they are prepared to put in to make sure that your business is a success. Indeed, as your business grows, its future success directly depends on having the right mix of people with the right skills. If you are serious about growth, you want your staff to be individually motivated, and keen to work together as a team. This means that you should know how to:

- analyse your job needs
- structure your organization to meet the demands of growth
- produce clear job descriptions
- find suitable staff
- decide when to recruit and when to train
- motivate your staff without losing control
- monitor performance effectively

If your business is growing, one of the most evident outward signs is often an increase in your workforce. In turn, this growth in staffing increases your need to have a clear idea of your workforce needs and to develop an organizational structure which is flexible enough to handle future growth. The technical and operational aspects of managing and recruiting staff are covered in *The Barclays Guide to Managing Staff for the Small Business* and, as it is an area criss-crossed with legislation and regulations, you will find some of the legal aspects dealt with in *The Barclays Guide to Law for the Small Business*. The main thrust of this chapter is to examine the principal organizational and management issues. Growing businesses are usually no strangers to organizational problems and often those problems are caused by the changing role of the owner as the business grows. It is fundamental to the art of management that you know what your own objectives are, before you consider introducing any genuine delegation or innovation. Once you have analysed your own principal business role, your next priority is to make sure that your entire business is organized for growth.

The main aim of this chapter is to provide you with a means of analysing your current and future job needs, so that you can develop an appropriate organizational structure for your growing business. To do this effectively, you need to be able to develop a system of genuine delegation (responsibilities not merely tasks) and the ability to write clear and succinct job descriptions. You also need to be able to decide if new skills should be trained in-house or bought in and how to motivate your workforce. Finally, you need to develop the necessary skills for running effective meetings. These areas are covered in detail under the following headings.

Analysing your job requirements

There are two main considerations to bear in mind when thinking about reorganizing your firm – personal objectives and organizational needs. The first involves you in thinking about yourself, how you see your role in the firm, and what you want to achieve personally in relation to your business. Essentially, this means that you have to define your own job, both at present and in the future, and this is not as easy as it sounds. To define your own job accurately, you have to identify what you actually do currently – the tasks you prefer to do, those you feel you must do, and those you avoid – and what you feel you should be doing in the future. Because much of your business strategy ultimately depends on your personal business objectives and your attitudes to your business growth, your definition of your own job is the fundamental starting point for any analysis of how you should be organizing your business to cope with the strains of current and future growth.

Secondly, you have to analyse what the commercial and organizational needs of your business are in relation to its best path for expansion. Basically, this means taking into account the financial (see chapter 6) and marketing (see chapter 7) environment in which you currently operate. In organizational terms, this means that you should closely examine your present strengths and weaknesses in relation to where you want your business to go and what you want it to be in the near future (say one to five years, depending on your business and the markets that you trade in). The next, and fairly demanding, step is to analyse and redefine jobs according to the tasks and responsibilities likely to be in demand during the coming year. Finally, you have to design a structure that is sufficiently robust to deal efficiently with sudden increases in your routine business transactions yet sufficiently flexible for you to respond rapidly to any new opportunities or sudden shifts in customer demand.

By now, you should have a clear idea of your own personal qualities in relation to your business. You should also be reasonably aware of your own personal business goals. Furthermore, it should also be clear by now that even the most minor changes to your firm will have to involve the effective delegation of some of your tasks and authority to other people in the firm. Effective delegation means more than just delegating tasks; it has to include giving, within clearly described limits, genuine autonomy of responsibility and authority. Starting with yourself, then together with each key employee or group of workers:

- Try to describe briefly each person's job
- List all the tasks and responsibilities which are necessary for doing the job well
- Try to sort the tasks and responsibilities into those which you consider to be central to the job and those which are not essential
- List any extra tasks and responsibilities that you feel your business needs in order to cope successfully with its likely growth over the coming year
- List the sorts of people the employee will come into contact with and note any special characteristics of the job (e.g., shift work, unsocial hours, unpleasant conditions)
- Note the tasks which are routine and those which require some independent judgement and responsibility for their completion
- Group the tasks into different broad areas of function and responsibilities
- Agree with your key staff on their areas of responsibility and the

tasks and responsibilities of the jobs within each area of functional responsibility

It may be that you can instantly see from these lists how to bring more order to the mix of tasks and responsibilities which make up the job descriptions of the people who work in your firm. If you find it a bit tricky analysing all the jobs, remember that, apart from tasks and responsibilities, you must look at the things that people do. If you do discuss your employees' jobs with them, you may be surprised to find that you do not share the same priorities. You can analyse their normal work routine according to what they do, and when, why, where and how they do the things they do, according to how you think it should be and how they tell you it really is. Finally, you can do the same to yourself by discussing your work with someone you know and trust.

Effective reorganization will require at least two concrete steps: a job-needs analysis and the drawing of an organizational chart (see Exhibit 2.1). Although both these steps sound rather formal, you will find that the ground has already been prepared. The important point to keep in mind is that your new job specifications and organization must be flexible for future change, yet geared to the production of your present most profitable product.

The job-needs analysis is simply a method you can use to identify which jobs are required for the effective management of your business and production of your products – manufacturing, service or retail. Your aim is to promote efficiency and deter overloading by allocating clearly defined tasks and responsibilities to appropriate members of your workforce (and to identify jobs for which you may need to recruit or train people). Basically, the analysis consists of listing the jobs and functions that actually exist and comparing them with those you feel that your business needs, if it is to meet the objectives that you have in mind.

If there are any significant mismatches between the jobs that you analysed as being central to your business and how you or your key employees actually spend the time, then you have a strong clue on where you are due for a reorganization. The areas that you identified as time wasters (in chapter 3) should also give you a strong clue on where your business could benefit from some reorganization. To see how important this analysis is to your business, work out which of your own tasks and functions should have priority to ensure the smooth running of your business. Then decide what changes you will have to make to your own working practices or areas of direct responsibility to ensure that you do in fact meet your own priorities. Repeat the analysis with each of your key workers and rewrite the job descriptions (see pp. 50–3), avoiding overlaps and making sure that neither you nor your key employees are too tied up with routine tasks.

Of course, apart from any legal constraints, there are a number of other considerations you have to take into account when redesigning jobs, for instance, the individual abilities and objectives of the people working for you. We shall examine these in more detail in a later section. It is worth pointing out that your task of redesigning jobs will be made much easier if you involve those most affected by your plans in the project of identifying new jobs or redesigning old ones. It will pay in the long run to find some way of getting comment and feedback from your workforce.

Also, you have to keep in mind at all times the actual resources – human, physical and financial – that you have at your disposal, or that you could realistically acquire within the time frame that you are planning for. These resources will include the materials and machines as well as the number of people involved, how much space is used and how much time is required. You will also have to think about who should be responsible for each step and who they have to deal with, and, of course, do not forget to estimate your likely gains in efficiency and profitability.

Structuring your organization

Job descriptions, job-needs analysis and other techniques for analysing what everyone in your business actually does (including yourself) are, however, only the beginning. If you were spurred into action by the confusion and chaos that often accompanies unplanned growth, then your real objective should be to find a new organizational structure for your expanding business. Apart from the obvious need for everyone to know everyone else's duties and responsibilities, any reorganization should be conducted so that it not only improves the efficiency of your business but also controls the flow of important information. Also, a restructuring can have profound financial and legal implications – especially if you started your business as a sole-trader or partner and now feel that a switch to being a limited liability company is in your best interests. These aspects are covered thoroughly in *The Barclays Guide to Financial Management for the Small Business* and *The Barclays Guide to Law for the Small Business*, though you should be aware that both the legal and financial implications of any reorganization will also add to your need to manage the storage and flow of information efficiently.

Of course, how your business is structured and how business information is processed are two closely related issues which, as businesses grow, depend increasingly on how successfully the owner has managed to delegate genuinely not just tasks but responsibilities also. No growing business can hope to function anywhere near top efficiency if the chief decision-maker feels obliged to deal in person with every aspect of the business. This is not just a question of efficient time management – although it is a crucial element in the successful management of time – but a more fundamental question about business priorities and the appropriate use of resources. As a business grows, the owner should be spending more time on planning and strategic issues. Owners who are reluctant to delegate the running of certain parts of their business to other people run the risk of drowning in a flood of low-level information and losing sight of their own objectives. Ultimately, business efficiency demands that an owner steps back from the day-to-day routine of the business, if that business is not to perish.

Standards of efficiency will vary according to the size and nature of your business but most businesses do have some central functions that are similar. For instance, our two fictional examples – the small engineering firm Batchjob and the small computer services firm Compburo – will both depend strongly on having well-run offices, even though Compburo designers work in a markedly different environment from that of the shop floor of Batchjob. Also, Compburo may need a minimum set of reference books and specialist magazines but not the stores or delivery sections required by Batchjob to fulfil the just-in-time requirements of its main contractors. Control of resources such as specialist information or reference material could form part of the main office or may be a separate function, depending on the particular nature of the business. Likewise, stock control or despatch could also be the responsibility of the main administrative office, although in a growing business these would soon become separate functions.

Indeed, as most businesses grow, separate functions tend to require their own individual organization with their own areas of responsibility. In smaller firms, 'the office' often refers to where the owner and an administrative assistant work. Whether the administrative assistant is a full- or part-time secretary, book-keeper, clerk or non-specified member of the owner's family, a common division of labour is for the owner to take business decisions, handle serious problems and conduct negotiations, while the assistant makes sure that wages and petty cash are attended to, that there is a note of any orders or appointments and that letters get typed and filed. In a very small firm, the efficiency with which the office is organized, how much work the owner and other members of staff get through and how well the main products are sold all depend on the competence of the individuals concerned.

As businesses grow – whether they offer services, help distribute other people's products or actually process products themselves – success and growth depend more and more on how efficiently each separate function is organized and how efficiently the main office can process the information that is necessary to control and co-ordinate the various activities in the business. The orderly management of growth increasingly reflects how efficiently the main co-ordinating office is organized. In this context, efficiency means producing what is expected, no more and no less, for the minimum expenditure of time, effort and money.

As the business grows, certain tasks performed by either the owner or the assistant figure become important enough or time-consuming enough to become a function in their own right. The small, ill-defined office should begin to shed these expanding, non-central tasks. At the same time, however, the number and variety of records and files will also increase with growth. More people will need to be paid and people will expect to take their holidays at different times of the year. The number of different types of appointments for different people will also increase – sales appointments, company representatives, VAT or tax inspectors, new customers, new suppliers, recruitment interviews, and so on – as will the number of meetings to be arranged (both internal and external). If the owner has been fairly successful at delegating some of the key functions, each of the people in charge of the different areas will require a different set of information and different records. The net result is that the main office also grows even bigger, despite having hived off many of its earlier functions (such as stock control, sales, delivery, maintenance, planning, and so on).

Question 11   In what way has your office changed as your business has grown? Do you feel that information currently flows in and out of your present office in the most efficient ways that it could?

Even though most businesses feel themselves to be unique and are, in fact, individually different from other businesses, the process of growth almost invariably leads to the development of separate functions and the growth of the office as a central coordinating and administrative function. As mentioned in chapter 3, as you begin to respond to growth by delegating tasks and, later, by genuinely delegating responsibilities, you will rely more and more on the central office for feedback and monitoring the overall performance of your business. It is essential that the core administration of your business is properly organized to serve the needs of your growing business.

Above all, a well-run office has to have an appropriate system for storing and retrieving information. In a growing business the storage and retrieval system has to be capable of rapid expansion and of rapidly providing the information required by different people for a variety of purposes. Rigid systems should have no place in most small firms and no place in growing business. The precise system will, of course, depend on a number of factors such as the volume of transactions, the quantity of items stored, the speed required for retrieval, the level of detail required in records and vulnerability to hazards such as fire, water, theft or fraud. If you or your administrative assistant do not have much time to spend in designing your own system, there are plenty of commercial systems available.

Most information processed by most offices is relatively common-place – customer enquiries, written orders, telephone or fax orders, invoices, receipts, payments of accounts, financial ledgers, business correspondence, sales contacts, communications from the VAT office, local authority or taxation authorities (and your or your accountant's replies), complaints, bills for running expenses, customer records, relevant publications or trade brochures. Many businesses will also need to handle a number of other, less common items of information as well as internal employment records, stock inventories, memos and, most importantly, customer enquiries and complaints (plus have a system for responding rapidly to both). With so much functional information passing in and out, it is sometimes easy to forget that the office in a growing business may also increasingly become the first point of contact between the business and important customers, suppliers and even new staff. Consequently, the office – especially if it is also the main reception area – may also need to be attractive. Frequently, the office also holds an internal telephone exchange, which means that the office staff should have some training in or guidelines on how to respond to telephone calls (which may also be the first point of contact with your business for outsiders). In any case, for security reasons, it is wise to locate your office near the main entrance/exit, and it will need to be large enough to accommodate all its records and staff without contravening any health and safety or fire regulations. Remember that the information stored in your office is, increasingly, your basis for controlling and monitoring your business.

Producing clear job descriptions

As the term implies, a job description is basically an outline of the tasks, duties and lines of responsibility that define a job. Its fundamental value lies in clarifying where various members of staff – including yourself – stand in relation to each other, but it is also essential in drawing up terms and conditions of work and in design-ing effective job advertisements. If your business were static, you could afford to develop job descriptions which encourage maximum output for a profitably minimum number of jobs. However, assuming that your business is expanding, you should ensure that your job descriptions allow for reasonable flexibility.

Of course, you do need to be aware of any legal constraints (and if you are using your job descriptions for recruitment advertising, you would be well advised to read the relevant sections in *The Barclays Guide to Law for the Small Business*). There are also a number of other considerations that you have to take into account when re-designing jobs. The most important of these relate to the individual abilities and objectives of the people working for you. We shall examine these in more detail in the next section, but one point is worth making. Because job descriptions define the positions and general tasks expected of each person in your business, make sure that the people affected agree and understand that the eventual descriptions do reasonably represent their jobs and that they do clearly define their working relationships with other people in the business. If you think they are under a misapprehension as to what their job or role is, save yourself from future problems by clearing up the matter.

There are many different methods which can be used for arriving at useful job descriptions and few organizations get it right first time. However, the lists of tasks, duties and functions that you produced in analysing your job requirements (p. 44) are probably the best start. As a check, however, think through the flow of tasks that are necessary for the production of your most important product. Make sure that you are satisfied that the new job descriptions are more effective than the old way. The basic information to include in a job description is listed in Exhibit 4.1.

Job title

Main purpose of the job

Principal duties and responsibilities (detailing key tasks)

Location (department, office location, split location, etc.)

Reporting line

Authority and accountability (of the post-holder over assets, spending, and people)

Key contacts (internal and external)

Working conditions (place, times, special environment)

Problems and constraints

Exhibit 4.1 Outline of a typical job description

Some managers criticize the use of job descriptions, claiming that they can be unhelpful and can rapidly become out of date. The key point is that even in the most flexible of organizations people need to know what they are trying to achieve and, ultimately, how to allocate costs. Hence some indication within a job description of the purpose of the job, together with key areas of responsibility and authority, is essential if the person doing that job is to have any chance of success, or indeed if your business is to survive for long. Also, if you are to have any chance of selecting the right person for the job, it is essential to know exactly what role the candidate has to fulfil within your business and for the right type of candidate to identify him or herself through the job description and come forward and apply for the job. Consequently, it is vital, from a management point of view as well as for organizational considerations, to be able to identify the right jobs and to be able to describe them accurately. You will find this important area covered thoroughly in *The Barclays Guide to Managing Staff for the Small Business*.

From a management viewpoint, however, it is worth while remembering that growth in a smaller firm usually means that flexibility is of paramount importance, so your job descriptions should be drawn up to reflect the changing nature of your business environment. One useful trick is to include a very general statement such as 'any other duties as and when required' in any job advertisements. However, you should be aware in your own mind that a job description does reflect the actual work undertaken by each member of staff and therefore sets a performance measure against which they will compare their performance. For this reason it is as well to make it as accurate as possible to avoid confusion and ensure that everyone has a similar perception of the job. This could be crucial in appraising performance, defining the limits and specifications of a new job or terminating a contract.

Having clearly described a job and the tasks to be done within it, your next step is to describe the kind of person you will need to do it. Drawing up a personnel specification is an essential part of the early recruitment and selection process. You will find it difficult to prepare a job advertisement, brief a recruitment agency, or prepare details about the job (further particulars) for prospective candidates without having a clear idea of the person you think would and could do the job. The purpose of this process is to provide you with a bench mark against which to assess the people who apply for the job. If you are unclear before an interview about either the job that you want done or the sort of person you want to do it, you will have substantially increased your chances of recruiting a person who is not suitable for the job or who may not fit in with your existing team.

Recruit or train?

Having defined the jobs, duties and lines of responsibilities in your new growth-oriented structure, the major (and rather time-consuming) problem of how to fill the various job slots satisfactorily remains. In most regions and industries, the problem of finding suitable staff has been growing for a number of years, mainly because of Britain's poor record at providing training for all levels of business (including management training). Apart from limiting the pool of trained or skilled workers (which will ultimately push up the cost of trained staff), this lack of training encourages some businesses to obtain their skilled labour from other firms. Unfortunately, smaller firms often end up being the victims of this tendency to recruit by poaching. Nevertheless, you should not let the fear of poaching deter you from trying to obtain the skills that your business needs to sustain growth by training your existing workforce. In general, poaching does make it harder for employers to introduce any form of training, except that which is highly specific to their own businesses. However, this fear of poaching cannot extend to your own training in management skills, and should not extend to people who have helped you build your business. In fact, planning a training programme for such people (and other suitable, newer employees) offers your staff the real chance of a career progression and helps to promote the image of your business as a professional place at which to work. We will return to this theme in chapter 8 when the issues of future growth are discussed.

However, even if you do not want your business to grow too large, there are still tangible benefits in introducing a policy of 'train and promote' rather than 'buy in' to acquire the skills that you have identified as being necessary to the future prosperity of your business. If you can identify an existing employee to transfer or promote, you benefit from their experience of your business and familiarity with company practices. You should also have a good (and, hopefully, objective) idea of their strengths and weaknesses. There is no doubt, too, that genuine promotion prospects act as an incentive to motivate staff. However, you should be careful to manage some of the difficulties that can arise in the relations that the newly promoted person may have with their former workmates or with established people on the same level.

You will have to make it perfectly clear from the start that the newly promoted person enjoys your full confidence. This sounds easy but can initially be difficult because it is unlikely that the person will be instantly in a position to perform the new tasks to your full satisfaction. It is usually the case that people are promoted because they are good at performing their existing jobs and there is often an expectation that employees will continue to perform in the new jobs as well as they did previously. You will have to make allowances for learning and settling in. You will also need to deal carefully and tactfully with those who have been overlooked, explaining your reasons to avoid misunderstanding and demotivation. In a small company, team work is essential.

If your firm is growing, finding the proper staff is even more difficult but, if the growth offers some range of career opportunities for your workers, then the problem of retaining good staff may ease off. Unfortunately, one of the main problems of growth is that it is very hard to find any time for planning or training, so it is also hard to find time to think about what promotion and career opportunities you may be able to offer and, perhaps, equally hard to communicate this to your workforce. However, it would be a mistake to think that training only exists to upgrade under-achievers. Indeed, training would be very expensive if its benefits were mainly confined to increased job satisfaction. Growing businesses begin to need a wider range of skills and, increasingly often, those skills are not in good supply or else are rather expensive to recruit. There are a wide range of vocational, technical and management training courses and programmes currently on offer which represents an important opportunity for smaller firms, because training offers the growing business a chance to construct its own dedicated team. However, for your growing business to reap the full benefits of training, it is best to have a systematic approach. Everyone in your business must have a clear idea of the intended benefits and how improved performance is to be measured.

For a growing business like yours, the overall objectives are simple. Whatever training you introduce or encourage should be aimed at increasing the level and range of technical skills, improving the performance of your existing employees, cutting down the learning time of newly recruited employees and preparing employees to take on future responsibilities, by boosting their capabilities and their self-confidence. To be of use to you, these benefits of training must more than offset the costs of time, money and disruption. How you achieve these objectives will depend on your business, the range of skills needed, your plans for the future and the individual aspirations of your employees. In other words, your training needs will be geared to your particular business and your business objectives. It may be that you want to limit your business growth to achieve a particular standard of living and life style and that the material covered so far is sufficient for you to arrange the appropriate level of training. If you intend to grow still further, however, you will need a more systematic approach to all your training – for both technical skills and management skills. The importance of training for future growth is a key issue addressed in chapter 9. For the moment, it is worth repeating that only by conducting an analysis of your present and future job needs will you be able to plan your training needs.

However, training will not solve your immediate lack of necessary skills if your growth has been rapid and your business lacks some fundamental technical or managerial expertise. If you feel that you are in this type of situation, you have to take a fairly urgent decision as to whether to recruit the skills that you lack, or train your existing staff in the required skills. To repeat, you must take into account the cost of the training itself, the cost of the time while staff are being trained and possible disruption from staff who are not being trained. Also you may have to come to grips with the biggest fear of small businesses – the risk that the freshly trained staff will immediately seek better-paid jobs elsewhere for their new skills. Against this, however, providing career paths and opportunities for self-improvement through training will act as an incentive for many of your employees. If you have been successful in creating an atmosphere where your employees feel involved in your firm, they are less likely to leave. Also, the costs of training can be offset against the costs of recruitment. Finally, training existing employees rather than recruiting will save you paying for a lot of learning time which new recruits will need before they are sufficiently familiar with your way of operating.

If you have decided that staff training is right for your firm, then you must decide how you are going to provide it. In previous years, many small business owners felt that the time taken for training was disruptive and costly, especially if the training was conducted off site. More recently, however, the range of all forms of training – technical, vocational and managerial – has expanded enormously and most (but be careful because not *all*) training providers do make serious efforts to provide value for money. There are now plenty of schemes operated through local colleges or enterprise agencies and a growing band of small-business training consultants.

Even more conveniently, depending on your objectives, a number of open- or distance-learning packages have been developed – including those of the Open University – which will enable certain skills to be taught at home or at work. Contact addresses and telephone numbers of local providers of training appropriate for smaller, growing businesses – including distance learning for managers – can be obtained from the local office of the Employment Department, a local Enterprise Agency or Chamber of Commerce or, sometimes, from the business department of a local college. Indeed, your local library can often be a useful place to start. The most appropriate form of training depends on the skills to be acquired. Often, the suppliers of expensive new machines will organize training either on site in your business or off site at a specially set-up training workshop. This training can be provided free and the level of instruction generally rises with the cost of the machine. On the other hand, if you are trying to organize your workforce in teams, or provide social-skills training for your supervisors and managers, or sales training for your sales staff, management consultants can arrange training sessions either on or off site, though the costs can be considerable.

Somewhere in between these two, government agencies, government-supported bodies (including colleges) and private companies offer training in a wide range of general managerial or business skills. Generally speaking, these are not expensive and you can often arrange for your employees to be taken as a group. Apart from complex machine skills training, most types of training are also available in open-learning format for individual study. Again, these courses are not expensive and they have the advantage that the training can take place at times which do not disrupt work. However, some skills training is more effective and more supportive if done in groups, so, if you are considering using open-learning packages, you might try using them with groups of employees rather than individually. Despite the fairly wide range of different training packages, however, it may be that you feel that training will take up too many current resources or that it will take too long to fill an immediate need. In these cases, you will need to recruit someone and you should make sure that you go about it in the right way so that you avoid wasting too much time initially – and later, if your original choice turns out to be a mistake.

There are a number of other reasonable sources of potentially well-motivated people who are looking for jobs, so poaching need only be considered as a last resort. If you are going to advertise, make sure that your advertisement is placed in the right place (local or national press, specialist magazines, trade press, local radio or TV or on suitable notice-boards) and that it includes all the key points in the job description. Before advertising for the job, however, there are a number of other sources of new staff worth exploring. The most common and least formal is word of mouth – from friends, colleagues, former employees, competitors, suppliers, and so on – which can be very effective if you trust your sources of information. Also, you should not reject previous applicants, casual enquiries, job centres, employment agencies, selection consultants, schools, colleges, universities and people who advertise seeking jobs.

However, even if you clearly identify the best source of recruitment from the choice available, this will not overcome any weaknesses in the job descriptions or person specifications nor any incompetence or prejudice which you allow to creep into any other part of the overall selection process. Every job recruitment will be different from those before, even if your business has had a similar or even identical vacancy in the past.

Question 12   Are you satisfied with how you have recruited in the past? Can you think of any lessons learnt from previous

occasions that might increase your chances of selecting the right person (or people) more efficiently?

If you are about to recruit for a new job, do stop to think before repeating your previous recruitment process. A different approach may be justified on this occasion. A different mix of recruitment techniques and sources of personnel may be relevant to your particular vacancy. It may pay you to weigh up the cost and time involved against the potential investment made in that new staff member. Remember that a poor recruitment decision will eventually cost your business money. Some of the suggested recruitment sources are free, some cost you money only when a successful appointment is made and others could cost you considerable amounts up-front, even before any results are seen. You will need to consider all these factors and weigh them up according to the specific nature of the job you have to fill, and the nature of your business.

Indeed, if costs and cash-flow implications are currently important you may not have to appoint a full-time employee, with all the costs that are involved, if you take the time to think through the job-needs analysis and consider all of the alternatives. While you are thinking through the options or analysing your job needs, you can always solve your immediate organizational problems by using part-time staff, temporary workers or, if they are amenable, turning to members of your family. However, it should be admitted that employing your family may not be the best permanent solution, but their support, understanding and commitment can help if you are not confident that taking on the additional person can be justified. Your preferred option will depend on your job needs and the willingness of your existing workforce to accept the arrangements, as well as your available resources and business objectives.

Indeed, if you are thinking about increasing your staffing levels by taking on more freelancers or part-timers, there are a number of issues to consider. First, temporary staff do increase your flexibility because you can alter the mix of skills to meet your different needs throughout the year and, often, it is possible to recruit multi-skilled part-timers. However, you should offer any chances of making extra money or changing work patterns to your existing staff first. If you can encourage your staff to work harder or to cover the additional work to match increasing levels of production, you could save money, and your staff may enjoy taking on the responsibility. Whatever you do, you must be seen to be acting fairly and even-handedly. If you are growing, and if growth has put some strains on your total organization, it is particularly important that your workforce believe in you and your integrity. This means that you pay part-timers or existing staff an agreed fee for an agreed job but, with freelancers, you are not responsible for national insurance contributions, holiday or sick pay, pensions, provision of maternity leave, or training. Apart from other Barclays Guides, more precise and current details can be found in a number of useful publications and leaflets – most of which should be available in your local library – published by such bodies as the Small Firms Service, the Advisory Conciliation and Arbitration Service (ACAS) and even the Inland Revenue.

Also, even if your longer-term aim is to recruit a permanent member of staff, hiring a freelancer or part-timer can still be a good idea if you can use the occasion as an opportunity to test how well that person or service fits with your company. However, there are disadvantages that you should be aware of. If the job involves a skill which is in short supply but for which there is a high demand, the fee may be considerably more than you would pay to an employee. You may find that temporary people are less enthusiastic than your own employees and, in addition, they are likely to be unfamiliar with your operations and standards, resulting in problems of discipline as well as motivation. On the other hand, even if you decide not to increase the size of your workforce but offer, instead, your existing staff the chance to make extra money through overtime, you may create new organizational problems.

It is a matter of judgement when the need for overtime becomes a need for an additional person. A workforce that is continually stretched finds it harder to respond quickly to urgent orders or a sudden peak in production. Overtime should be seen as an opportunity to offer staff a bonus for completing a job. The danger for both the employer and employee is that overtime becomes the norm and creates what are, in effect, unreasonable expectations. It can then be an expensive alternative for the employer and demotivating for the employee, particularly when the wages return to non-overtime levels. Once again, the questions of control and motivation appear and they will appear more frequently the more your business grows.

Controlling your workforce

It cannot be stressed too strongly that it is your system of control which lies at the heart of your organizational structure. You can have all the employee participation that you want and all the warm supportive atmosphere, but without control you have no real system – no real management. For delegation to work properly, you have to maintain a system of checks, so that you are kept informed, well in advance, of the important things happening in your business. In other words, you delegate genuine authority in certain areas, but only in exchange for precise responsibilities which include, amongst other things, the duty to keep you in the picture.

Likewise, the people to whom you have delegated authority have to make sure that they are kept informed of what is happening in their area. In fact, the process is not only one way. When you come to a decision, either by yourself or in consultation with a manager, your manager also has to ensure that the decision is implemented. Thus there is a dynamic process whereby your managers monitor the employees in their section to ensure that they are completing their usual tasks to a satisfactory standard, as well as responding to fresh decisions. These managers also report back to you the progress and problems associated with the employees in their section. You learn about the results of your decisions through your contact with your managers and these, in turn, are part of the information used to make succeeding decisions and to set future performance targets.

Targets set for personal performances must be measurable, achievable and fair. You must ensure that staff performance is regularly monitored and, where things have gone wrong, that corrective action is taken. At the same time you must listen to and communicate with your staff because they are frequently trying to give you warning signals about problems. As a result of listening to them you may need to review the whole process of setting targets and reviewing performance. With agreed targets and objectives, which are easily measurable, the monitoring process may consist of budgetary control, regular monitoring or performance reviews at set intervals. Indeed, having responsibility for a budget gives a sure sign to your key staff that their delegated duties and responsibilities are genuine.

For instance, if you give a member of staff responsibility for a certain budget (advertising, sales, administration or whatever), the budgetary control system should monitor the performance every month and the budget holder should provide reasons for under/over achievement of the budget and what remedial action is being taken. However, that member of staff should be given a free hand within the designated area of responsibility to ensure that targets are met. With regular reviews (weekly, monthly, quarterly, annual or seasonal), the past period's performance will be reviewed and new goals and targets set, or old ones continued and monitored. Where continual monitoring is essential for quality control, such as with assembly-line production or outworkers, actual performance is measured against present levels of acceptable performance (reject levels or agreed quality levels).

This system of management, which is only genuinely applicable if there is a means for measuring performance and a general agreement in advance that the targets set are reasonable, is fairly widely known as *management by objectives and results* (MOR). Obviously, the MOR system cannot work effectively where managers believe that they should set the objectives and dismiss their workers if they fail to achieve the expected results. Apart from anything else, the labour turnover rate would soon hit unacceptably high levels and the firm's reputation could sink to unpleasantly low levels. Also, if you intend to set limits to your growth, it may be that you will not have enough resources or tasks to be broken down into completely separate budgets and that the goals you agree with key members of staff will be less formal than stated objectives with set performance criteria. Still, if you do wish to continue to grow (an issue discussed more fully in chapter 8), it is essential to remember that the MOR system only works effectively if the objectives and means for measuring performance are realistic and agreed in advance.

There are a number of different methods of describing performance goals and measuring their attainment. Some larger companies talk in terms of *roles* and *missions* to describe the nature and scope of the work to be done, why the organization exists, and what resources it will commit to making it all happen. As you can see in chapter 8, roles, missions, performance goals and other similar management tools are very useful for developing a corporate image which, in turn, is very useful for maintaining morale and direction when your business grows beyond the point where you can have meaningful personal contact with all members of staff.

In fact, as a step along the path towards arriving at that stage of growth, dynamic firms and managers who are adept in the skills of planning will usually involve their immediate staff in developing special action plans to achieve special goals. Such goals, most of which are examined in more detail in chapter 8, could include the reorganization of their business, launching a new product, the relocation of the business, preparing for the Single Market and most other major activities that are likely to involve the entire firm. The contents of the action plan could include such activities as setting deadlines, allocating budgets, programming events, scheduling and deciding levels of responsibility, plus outlining how the objective will be achieved and at what cost.

There is no reason why a smaller firm cannot also refer to roles and missions or produce action plans but, in the first place, it is often more meaningful to identify *key results areas* upon which to focus. Typical areas for attention include productivity, cost control, personal production, unit production, profitability, sales turnover, orders or contracts of a certain type and customer enquiries. The essential features to keep in mind in deciding on your own key results area are that the area must be central to your business, capable of being improved and, most importantly, capable of being measured in some appropriate way. Indeed, as part of the process of identifying an area where the results are a key to your overall business performance you also need to identify a suitable *indicator* to use as an instant measure of effective or ineffective performance. Typical indicators include sales, profits, customer orders, enquiries, loads, machine output, ratios of total sales, ratios of costs, and others that are more appropriate to particular operations. Indicators should be measured in units that are easy to employ and sensitive to change. For instance, physical outputs could be measured in tonnes, ounces, pints, litres, gallons, yards, metres, container loads, pallets or whatever unit of measurement is standard in the particular industry. However, business indicators are more usually measured in money or in volume terms per unit, per sales staff, per production staff, per budget holder, per specified time period (hour, day, week, month, quarter, etc.), or in terms of percentage increase or decrease or whatever other form is appropriate.

Once you have decided which critical areas are the most appropriate and sensitive to monitor in your business and which indicators you intend to use, you will then have to decide the critical levels that indicate that your resources are being used to best effect. For instance, small engineers such as Batchjob know that some machines are not suitable for small-batch production and that they require a minimum level of activity to operate economically. Similarly, the high wages paid to skilled staff will be wasted if they spend too much time on low-skill activities. For example, Compburo would need a minimum number of CAD contracts to justify investing in their CAD equipment and employing their highly trained computer-based designer. As to the more financial indicators – such as financial ratios or similar measures – they can be compared with published industry norms and – more importantly – with your own past (and expected future) performance (see *The Barclays Guide to Financial Management for the Small Business* for a full description of how to calculate and use financial ratios), and critical levels are usually determined with reference to your objectives.

For these purposes, your measurement objectives should take the form of statements of measurable results (targets) to be achieved within the key results areas. For example, Batchjob might set an objective of increasing output per work hour by 10 per cent without loss of quality by the end of the year. There also might be an agreed sum in the budget (less than the expected increase in revenue) for achieving this target, which would effectively limit the range of options available. The target would have to be fair and achievable. Also, it would have to be agreed by the Batchjob supervisor and the shopfloor workers whose work practices could be affected by the new output target and whatever system of quality control may be needed. The indicator may be measured either in units per hour or in value of sales per hour (whichever is considered most appropriate for the business). Finally, the appropriate indicator can also be used to control various members of staff – both key staff with delegated areas of responsibility and their subordinates – by monitoring performance against objectives.

Of course, there is nothing to prevent you from accompanying one of your managers to see how a decision is implemented at first hand. However, you should always let the manager know in advance, and refrain from making any criticisms in front of the employees.

Also, you should not appear to be doing your manager's job as you do not want to undermine the manager's authority. Indeed, one of your own main tasks for which you should accept overall responsibility is to bolster the morale of both your managers and your workforce. As your business grows, the pressure on you to maintain motivation also grows more intense. For the system to work smoothly, you have to treat your managers as your eyes and ears – they are your early warning system. You also have to make sure that all your employees feel personally committed to your business.

Maintaining motivation

A lot of time and effort has been devoted to studying the connections between needs, wants, motivation, satisfaction and, ultimately, performance. Many of the findings are contradictory and what may be true for your business may not hold for a different kind of business round the corner or for a similar business in another part of the country. However, it does seem well established that people are motivated if they think that a proposed activity is likely to bring them satisfaction, and they are prepared to lift their performance if that potential satisfaction is sufficiently important to them. Naturally, few members of your staff (yourself included) will gain precisely the same satisfaction from the same outcomes, but it is, nevertheless, possible to generalize about different levels of satisfaction that most people appear to seek.

All people, from the prince to the pauper, have basic physiological needs to satisfy – hunger, thirst, warmth, and so on – and most people need to feel relatively safe and secure physically and psychologically. For most of the world these remain the main motivations to work. Once these basic needs have been satisfied, people start to become more diverse. At the next level of motivation, there is a need for social support and contact but this can take many different forms, and for the higher human needs – status, respect, power, etc. – the sources of satisfaction are endless. At the highest level, with the more inner personal needs to feel worth while and self-fulfilled, the goals and satisfactions are unique to the individual. Mostly, motivational issues at work concern the mid-level social needs and needs for status and power. Because, at this level, everyone has their own profile of needs and will satisfy those needs in their own way – not necessarily related to the size of their pay packet (unless, perhaps, when pay is seen generally as a measure of status) – incentives have to work on a number of different levels if they are to be effective.

Of course, on a more general level, there is a basic mimimum in pay and conditions that you have to provide your staff with before you can expect even average output, let alone strong commitment. If your business is growing, you should keep yourself up to date on the prevailing rates of pay for your industry in your district. The shortage of good, well-qualified labour is already quite acute in some areas and is expected to worsen – especially in the more highly skilled jobs. Contrary to some commonly held beliefs about motivation, pay is not always top of the list of incentives for achieving high motivation and output. However, low pay is very clearly a powerful disincentive and an obvious barrier to full staff commitment. Also, for similar reasons, there is a certain basic standard to be expected in work conditions, most of which is anyway covered by health and safety regulations, building and fire regulations, by legislation in such areas as industrial relations, equal opportunities, and appropriate clauses in various factories acts and other similar laws (many of the details of these laws and regulations are covered in *The Barclays Guide to Law for the Small Business* and *The Barclays Guide to Managing Staff for the Small Business*).

You cannot hope to motivate other people in your business unless you offer them pay and conditions that are not obviously below the local average. Respect, feeling valued, a sense of involvement have all been shown to be powerful motivators and, in many cases (though not all), they can have a greater effect than offering extra money. The theory underlying all motivational techniques is that, among your employees' motives in life, they have some needs, wants, desires or preferences relating to work. You have to offer something which your employees believe will satisfy these work motives and be worth the extra effort. In other words, both the need and the expected satisfaction have to be strong enough to compensate for the harder work. There is considerable debate about which work satisfactions are the most important and, given the wide range of personal tastes involved, it is not very productive to try to be too specific. Nevertheless, while it is not clear whether satisfaction itself actually leads to increased work (it may be that the prospect of future satisfaction is a stronger motivator), there is stronger evidence that high motivation actually does improve performance.

Human beings are social creatures and one of the strongest psychological satisfactions that work provides is a sense of belonging. To foster these positive feelings and offset any negative feelings, you should do everything you can to boost the social role that work plays for your employees. For example, you should make sure that your office, or whoever keeps your staff records, sends birthday greetings to employees at the appropriate dates. Encourage the formation of sporting clubs. Organize or support the celebration of the usual seasonal festivities. Some people believe that work also provides a sense of identity. Whatever the strength or prevalence of these needs, it is clear that they can best be satisfied in the climate associated with an employee-centred management style. If you have adopted a more consultative approach with clear job definitions and genuine delegation, there is little more that you can do organizationally. However, your employees' feeling of involvement with your firm is not simply a question of organization – it is also emotional. For those that have been with you a long time, the connection will be historical, an important chunk of their own lives. For others, the psychological reasons mentioned above may well be important.

Some wants and needs, such as those for success or recognition, actually grow stronger the more they are satisfied. It may be a cliché, but it is true that 'nothing succeeds like success'. This is one reason why you should make a point of seeking out your employees to praise them publicly for jobs done well. At the same time, be wary of the reverse effect and try to avoid publicly criticizing your employees, unless you feel it is important to make an exemplary point. This is also why you should make sure, as much as possible, that each employee's job description takes into account that employee's special strengths and weaknesses.

In other words, you should try to build success into the job and make it hard for employees to fail. If you included your employees in the job analysis and development of your new organizational chart, you may already be aware of many of their aspirations and you may find that offering training sessions provides an excellent opportunity for boosting the employee's motivation. Although there is a risk that your newly trained employees will be poached by a larger firm – especially if your industry is suffering from shortages of skilled labour – there is strong evidence to suggest that training, even on-the-job, informal training, increases not only employee motivation but also the length of time employees are likely to stay with your firm and, generally, in the same sort of job.

Finally, it would be a mistake to ignore economic motivation just because certain psychological needs are sometimes more powerful. For instance, firms which operate profit-sharing schemes have a significantly better financial performance than firms which do not. Certainly, if you have a reputation for being a relatively poor payer, do not be surprised if your labour turnover and absenteeism rates go up as the quality of your workforce goes down. Of course, the situation inside each business – whether in manufacturing, service, retailing, wholesaling, transport or construction – is unique. This means that the operation of any bonus scheme, productivity deal, piecework rate or pay agreement will also be unique to each business. For instance, in manufacturing and certain types of services incentives can easily be tied to output; in other businesses, incentives for sales staff usually take the form of commission on sales volume or on the total value of an important order. In a retail operation, the buyer might also receive a commission on a successful line. Other examples include: promotion to a higher grade, the chance to represent the firm at a social function, presentation of an award, free membership of a club or association, special rates for a medical or insurance scheme, free or reduced-price holidays, or a company car. All these, and more, can be used as incentives, but not all incentive schemes are appropriate for every business and every type of employee.

First, they cannot be too general or otherwise they will come to be regarded as part of the general pay and conditions. Second, the incentive must be linked to the individual's own personal or group output. Third, there must be some accepted method for measuring an increase in output. Finally, in common with all motivational techniques, the employees have to feel that the incentive is worth the extra effort. It is important to keep in mind the effect of taxation on incentives. Financial incentives and many non-financial incentives must be included with total employee income and therefore attract taxation. Consequently, a bonus of less than 10 per cent, by the time taxation has bitten into it, may not be sufficient to spur your employees into extra effort. On the other hand, you have to feel that the extra effort will more than cover the cost of the incentive.

As a rough guide, you can estimate the costs and benefits of potential incentives by first calculating an estimate of the overall cost (based on your previous year's sales figures, your current projections and the number of workers likely to be receiving the incentive). Next, decide how you are going to measure any increase in performance and estimate the minimum boost to overall performance that you expect following the introduction of the incentive. Finally, estimate how much your profits will increase if the increase in performance reaches your minimum level and, if the cost of the incentive is below your expected increase in profits, start planning how to introduce the incentive. However, before doing so, you would be best advised to discuss the matter with the employees concerned, but only if you genuinely intend to introduce that incentive. If the incentive, the changed work practices or the method of measurement is not to their satisfaction, you may find that the proposed incentive has quite the opposite effect. If you talk about it but fail to follow through, you may weaken their trust in you.

A growing business needs to have everybody pulling together and having members of staff working below their capacity can disrupt other staff. Sometimes, however, incentives seem incapable of producing extra effort in certain employees who seem to be devoid of energy and interest. Nevertheless, there may be good grounds for resisting the temptation to dismiss under-achievers. Apart from any compensation you may have to pay, you also have to consider the costs of replacement, the disruptions in introducing new staff and the possible cost to your reputation as an employer. To a large extent *The Barclays Guide to Managing Staff for the Small Business* will help you tackle these issues, especially recruitment and how to get the right people without spending a fortune. But, even with efficient recruitment practices, you cannot avoid spending time and money on advertising, interviewing and monitoring the performance of every new employee. Furthermore, it is not only the actual time and money spent but also the cost of you, or your top staff, being kept away from more important matters. Of course, if you have managed to delegate effectively you will, to some extent, be insulated from the more routine personnel problems. However, if the under-achiever holds a relatively high position in your firm, the costs both of replacement and your time will also increase.

When considering the cost, you will also have to weigh up the present performance effects of the under-achiever on the rest of your workforce. Replacing the under-achiever means you will be faced with certain disruption as your workforce copes first with having to work under-staffed, and then with a new, inexperienced employee who has to learn how your business works. Before deciding on dismissal, therefore, it is best to examine how you might raise the under-achiever's performance. You first have to decide why the employee's performance is below what you expect. To start with, either you or the person immediately responsible should review the job description together with the employee and make sure that it is suitable and that the employee understands what the job entails. You all should be clear about what objectives need to be achieved, how performance is measured and that the employee has not reached the required performance level.

Depending on the circumstances, the review meeting could be either informal and supportive or else formal enough to satisfy the first stage of dismissal procedures. In any case, the employee should be given a chance to discuss any grievances or complaints. It may be that in clarifying any misunderstandings about the true objectives of the job, you have also solved the problem of under-achievement. However, if you feel that originally you may have misjudged the employee's level of ability or competence, then either redefine the job or else offer an alternative job more suitable to the employee's abilities.

On the other hand, if the employee does understand the objectives of the job and does not seem too incompetent to achieve them, you have to take another course of action. The most likely cause of the problem is that something, or someone, is interfering with the employee in the performance of the job. If the problem is a lack of knowledge or experience on the employee's part, then the solution is to provide advice or training. If the problem is emotional, then advice or counselling is appropriate. The employee's complaints or grievances should give you a clue. If the problem is one of social relations or working conditions, then you have a broader problem and you will have to return to your job organization programme. The problem may not be with the under-achiever but rather with another employee, or group of employees, or it may have to do with how the work is organized.

You, or whoever has overall responsibility – though not necessarily the person with immediate responsibility – should discuss the matter with all concerned, because it may be that the employee's under-achievement is a symptom of more serious problems in your firm. Lack of morale or motivation is frequently a sign of poor direction or communication. Even more fundamentally, under-achievement may really reflect incompetence or insensitivity – and not always of the under-achiever but perhaps of his or her immediate superior, or of the person responsible for organizing the workload (who may, in fact, be you). When you encounter under-achievement, first consider what you could do personally to improve the situation. If, after mature reflection, however, you decide that it really is a question of motivation and that your main problem is that of motivating the under-achiever, it boils down to finding out what motivates the employee. Do not forget that your employees may be at a different level of motivational need than you. During the session at which the problem is discussed with the employee, either you or the person responsible should endeavour to get an idea of what goals the employee has in your business and outside it. Again, the discussion of the employee's grievances or complaints should give you a clue and, of course, you should ask the employee directly. Do not be surprised to discover, however, that employees who perform low-level, routine jobs do not regard your business as the centre of their universe and actively resist participation.

After eliminating many of the obvious causes for below-par performance and introducing realistic work goals, you are in a strong position to tackle the problem of under-achievement. Indeed, even taking the time to discuss these matters with the employee can often do the trick. By mapping out a possible career path, or offering suitable incentives, you can further encourage the employee. Finally, by taking care to praise any achievements and restricting criticism to lack of effort rather than failure itself, you will have taken all the steps you could be reasonably expected to take to boost the under-achiever's self-confidence and performance. Chapter 8 deals with many of the issues connected with streamlining your organization for future growth, including how to rid your business of unwanted products, equipment and staff.

Summary

This chapter has looked at the heart of your organization and examined the main issues that you need to consider if you are to create the right structure for your growing business. Such a structure has to be sufficiently ordered to bring order into the chaos of unplanned growth yet flexible enough so as not to impede future growth. The main issues discussed related to the need of many growing businesses to conduct a proper analysis of their job needs, both current and future, then to construct an organization based on those needs and a system, through either recruitment or training or both, for meeting the future challenges of growth. The need to maintain the motivation of the growing workforce was also examined.

Key points

- Successful reorganization for growth means that you must analyse your job needs.
- The job specifications for those needs need to be clearly written.
- Structure your organization according to present skills and future needs.
- Involve your workforce in the restructuring and foster a feeling of identification with the fate of your business.
- Delegate not merely tasks but also responsibilities according to the principal functions in your business.
- Set clear objectives and yardsticks so that performance can be properly monitored and controlled.
- Try to use training to foster a sense of career development within your business.
- Relate incentives to real motivations and measurable performance outcomes.

5

Creating the space for growth

Outline

One aspect of growth and business success that is often overlooked is the importance of location and having the right premises. For service businesses especially, not only are the location and appearance of premises fundamental to the creation of the desired image but also payments relating to premises may be the single biggest item of capital expenditure. This chapter looks at:

- how to assess your current premises needs
- how to determine efficient use of your space
- the relative advantages of refurbishing and moving
- what to consider when leasing or buying

Once you have addressed the organizational aspects of growth, the next most evident, physical manifestation of unplanned growth is that you begin to run out of space. Basically, this can be due to a number of reasons, the most obvious of which is that your present premises are no longer big enough to house your expanded business. However, there are a couple of less obvious reasons. It may be that you are using your existing space inefficiently or it may be that you are conducting too many activities in your present premises. The aim of this chapter is to examine these issues and to identify the most appropriate solutions. Apart from moving to new premises, your range of options includes refurbishing your existing premises, re-designing your current use of space, acquiring additional premises, sub-contracting some of your activities or some of your storage, and just cutting back on some of your more space-consuming activities.

Identifying the most appropriate option or mix of options solves only part of the problem. You also need to know how to conduct a simple premises audit, so that you can anticipate future needs, and decide whether you should buy or lease (or go for a mixture of the two). These questions are addressed in the following sections.

Auditing your premises needs

Although increasing lack of space is one of the classic symptoms of growth, the exact form that space shortages take and the main reasons for overcrowding vary from one business to another. You may also find pressure on your existing space if your office staff grows and the increased office supplies begin to push your office workers into other parts of the premises. If you have a manufacturing business, the pressures on your stock control system will also grow as your sales and output increase. Many service businesses, particularly those that essentially offer skilled, trained, organized or dedicated labour (office cleaners, designers, employment agencies, nursing staff agencies, etc.), find that growth inevitably means recruiting more people thus increasing pressure on existing space.

Another side-issue connected with increased growth may be that your business has mainly grown in one area – for example, supplying parts or services to electronics manufacturers – and actually shrunk in others – for example, supplying parts or services to hospitals. Businesses are seldom static. The political, economic and technical climate surrounding them is changing, which affects the technology available to do their job, the markets they work in, the products they deal in and the activities they undertake. The result of this fluidity is a high rate of personnel turnover, shifts in the quality of staff employed, reorganizations of working groups and relationships, and possibly an increasing take-up of office automation. These changes are happening incrementally and are often unplanned for, with the result that in many businesses dramatic changes have occurred without a clear premises strategy.

Because premises can be relatively expensive, it does pay to spend some time considering how your premises impact on the rest of your business. Failure to do so often results in uneven space standards with gross overcrowding in key areas. Indeed, as you grow you are likely to experience a changing pattern of activities to space, as the spatial demands of new activities and equipment are felt. Casual planning (in effect no planning at all) is often reflected in inefficient use of space and disjointed relationships between parts of a business. Some service businesses suffer from a deteriorating visual, aural and climatic environment due to an increase in office automation equipment, with the inevitable spread of cables, and noise and heat. Ultimately, the hidden costs can surface as problems of unplanned growth leading to eventual loss of financial control.

To find out where you stand – especially if you feel that your growth up till now has been fairly random – you should take stock of how you are using space and how much of your space is being used efficiently. If you have been growing rapidly, you can probably already identify the areas of your business that are most overcrowded and most in need of change. If, on the other hand, you have not had much time to identify your most pressing space constraints, it is not too difficult to conduct your own quick survey (or *space audit* as it is sometimes known). Simply measuring your total internal usable space – marking off the 'dead' areas (stairwells, cupboards, passages, corridors, toilets, etc.) – and dividing by the number of people using each room will give you a rough idea of your most densely crowded work areas.

If you know how much the prevailing annual rent per square metre (or square foot) is for your type of building, you can easily calculate your real cost of space per employee or per work area. If you feel that you need a more accurate assessment (if, for example, you are tossing up in your mind whether or not to move), you will need to test actual space usage against an effective space budget and your planned use of space. If you have a clear idea of what purposes you need your different work areas for and how many people you plan to employ in each area, it should be relatively easy to estimate your budgeted space requirements to support your future plans for growth. For instance, your planned use of new technology may lead to certain changes. If you are currently using computers or thinking about doing so, conducting a space audit should help you review the changing demands of your business in the light of the take-up of information technology.

This section first sets out the various definitions used in analysing space, to ensure that we are comparing like with like. Secondly, it identifies the criteria to apply when assessing the effectiveness of a building in meeting your requirements. However you husband the use of space available, few inroads may be made into operating costs if the building shell contains inbuilt inefficiencies which provide a poor ratio of usable space to gross area, so dramatically increasing cleaning, maintenance, heating costs and so on. Lastly, we look at simple ways of periodically assessing that space is being used effectively.

In assessing the space required by your business, you need to decide not only a reasonable estimate of the amount of space needed by your staff to complete their work satisfactorily but also the ancillary areas that a business like yours normally needs. For instance, the workplace area – which could be either enclosed or open-plan – could include desks, filing, meeting spaces, individual computer terminals and so on. The ancillary areas are for core activities that support more than one workplace. Frequently, this space is shared or owned and managed by different groups (such as group adminis-tration, filing, mainframe computer terminals or meeting space). In addition, you need to take into account *secondary circulation routes* and support areas. For ease of planning, secondary circulation routes are often included in workplace standards and are valuable when measuring the efficiency of space usage. Support areas, which may be divided into auxiliary spaces and special spaces, are usually required for functions which are more central to the operation of your business as a whole. In many buildings you cannot avoid the auxiliary spaces that are essential to running the building (for example, workshop, cleaning, goods area). Also, if your business has a need for special spaces (for instance, display rooms, labora-tories, entertainment areas, etc.), you will need to take these into account.

In establishing a *space budget* – the total amount of floor space you require – it may be useful to use simple rules of thumb, giving areas required per office staff member. This could be expressed according to several of the above definitions. Typically, when assessing existing layouts it will be expressed either as designed office area per staff member (workplace plus ancillary plus secondary circulation) or designed usable area per staff member (designed office area plus support). When assessing the space available in a building, you might expect to find that your net internal area is roughly three quarters of your gross internal area while your actual usable area is again roughly three quarters of your net internal area (up to one half of your gross internal area). These proportions may vary dramatically depending on the number, depth and configuration of floors.

At first sight, it may seem that this represents a terrible waste of space and, sometimes, it is rather space inefficient. However, there are a number of statutory regulations that commercial buildings have to comply with (health and safety, fire and building, and many others, including those specified in factory acts and other specific items of legislation) and it is more likely that many of the non-lettable areas in larger buildings are due to such factors as the need to provide means of escape, the sizing of lifts and width of stairs, the provision of toilets, the capacity of ducts and, in manufacturing and processing businesses, space for plant. In practice, the ratio of usable space to gross internal area may vary over similar-sized buildings, a point which should be well understood and not overlooked when reviewing your premises. In addition to assessing your premises according to their flexibility for planning, the capacity of building shells should also be assessed according to their potential to accommodate enclosed offices and their adaptability for different styles of layout, and size of working groups. Also, keeping your future computer and informational technology needs in mind (see *The Barclays Guide to Computing for the Small Business*) you should note the capacity of present and future premises to accommodate cables and the flexibility of any air conditioning to adapt to varying heat loads.

How much space your company needs to carry out its functions is, or should be, determined by your business plan. The future size and composition of your workforce, the areas that you decide are central to your main business activities, the image that you believe is right for your business and the premises that you feel you can afford can be summarized in a premises policy statement or at least a note that outlines your decisions and key issues in relation to your future premises needs. Indeed, taking all these considerations into account, you should be able to estimate an ideal or standard area of workspace for each type of employee. Once you have decided on your premises policy you can develop your own guidelines on the allocation of cellular offices, space standards and rules of thumb for support functions.

The space budget is the summation of the amount of space required for office space, support space and expansion space. The space budget is built up by multiplying the number of staff by the appropriate standards of space usage and then adding areas for support and expansion. The result is a space demand independent of the efficiency of a particular building. Building shells, according to their configuration, depth and planning grids, suggest planning principles to make the most effective use of the space provided. Leaving aside the actual building stock that you have to deal with, the smooth flow of your future growth will depend on how accurately you can establish space policies regarding the size and dimensions of office space, while taking account of relevant planning rules.

Efficient use of space

Basically, how efficiently you are using your present or will use your future premises depends on two broad factors – the organizational and the physical. First, you need to decide how efficiently the various areas of your business (administration, production, storage, and so on) are individually organized and whether the use of those different areas accurately reflects their importance to your overall business. Most of the issues connected with the effective organizational use of space were mentioned in chapter 4 (especially pp. 46–50 on structuring the organization). In relation to the second broad factor, the effective physical use of your space, the constraints and opportunities of the building should be analysed and suitable people: workspace density standards should be agreed.

When assessing the suitable space standards for different types of workspace you have to take into account health and safety regulations, design, comfort and image considerations, equipment manufacturers' recommendations, the efficiency of work flows and, above all, how your staff feel about layout and space. You then need to decide whether standards can be varied to meet the effective use of the building without impairing the efficiency of your operation. Organizations which apply rigid space policies about size of offices, allocation of enclosure and access to views may find themselves using space less and less effectively.

**Question 13   Do you currently have target standards (people:
workspace ratios)? Can you apply your current policy on the
amount and quality of space per person efficiently to all suitable
building areas?**

The objective in assessing how your space is being used is to relate
the amount of space you are in practice using to norms that exist for
firms in a similar business to your own. These norms, in addition to
reflecting lettable, usable and workplace area per person, may also
include a number of different grades, amount and type of enclosure
provided, average ancillary space per person, and number of staff
per meeting room. You should also assess the way space is being
used in practice against organizational guidelines and identify
discrepancies of space provision and usage between parts of the
company, people and groups of people. Space-planning guidelines
formulated by the organization may bear little relation to changes in
patterns of work and the technology used in some groups, and the
space audit may help to identify these discrepancies.

The quickest way of making an initial assessment of how effectively
space is being used is a plan survey. This first step, with the
minimum of input, allows an assessment to be made of the proportion
of space being used for circulation and support, and people space
which can be compared with company standards and expected
practice. A survey will also enable you to identify the average
workplace area per person in different departments and the size and
number of cellular offices. Using existing floor plans of the building,
a 'walk round' survey can be made of the building to note the
numbers of people in each room or area, members of staff per
machine (in service businesses this will be increasingly applicable
with the spread in use of computers, VDUs, printers, and so on) in
each space, easily identifiable ancillary activities and rooms with
specialist support functions.

First, measure each floor and then each room. Note how much
space is occupied by 'non-accommodation' areas such as corridors,
cupboards and stairwells. Calculate how much usable space you
have by subtracting all the space occupied by storage, passageways,
lift wells, stairs, walls and so on from your total space. Next calculate
your average space per person by dividing your usable space total by
the number of your employees (including yourself). You can then

work out how widely each room varies from that average. If you have wide variations then you are not using space efficiently. Also, you will have identified the rooms which are the least space-efficient and you can decide what you would prefer to do about improving their lay-out or usage. Only after completing your own space audit and premises survey (which you complete for your own managerial purposes, not as a professional structural survey) will you be in a position to allocate space efficiently or decide that new premises are needed. You will also be in a strong position to decide whether your new premises are to result from a redesign and refurbishment of your existing premises or a relocation to a new site (or even a mixture of the two).

Refurbish or relocate?

The most common first reaction to finding that your premises have become too small is to start looking for bigger premises elsewhere. However, lack of space may not be the only reason to contemplate a move. Uneven growth may have rendered your present location unsuitable, but, alternatively, your growth may have coincided with (or have been led by) a move up-market, and your original, cheap premises may now have become an image liability. In short, growth can produce effects on your premises needs – and your desire to move – other than the mere pressure of space.

Of course, relocating creates almost as many problems as un-planned growth, so you should be sure that you feel you have adequately addressed the various issues mentioned above before deciding to move. Indeed, an interim solution may be to acquire additional premises either for the office staff and your administration or for a particular part of your business (storage, delivery, production, etc.). In fact, this is how many firms do grow, especially services which find that it makes good business sense to exploit untapped markets in new localities. You may have a number of reasons for deciding to remain in existing space but to make use of it more efficiently. Moving to new premises can often mean higher rents and expenditure on fit-out and relocation allowances. Other reasons for not moving may include disruption to business and staff, loss of proximity to clients or reduced accessibility. Also, of course, moving is usually very disruptive. Having made the decision to remain, however, careful consideration will have to be given, immediately, to how to rectify the identified problem or problems and, in the longer term, how to obtain more efficient use of your premises.

The main purpose of conducting an audit of your current space usage is to provide yourself with relevant data and facts relating to all aspects and characteristics of your premises. A simple survey will reveal most of the key factors – the differential running costs of buildings, the drawbacks associated with certain locations, inefficient layouts caused by inflexible space, overcrowding and so on – that you need to be aware of to make informed decisions about your premises. What a simple survey does not usually provide, however, is a description of the performance of your premises measured against the overall requirements of your business. The premises policy that you adopt to cope with growth must ultimately depend on the business targets and longer-term objectives that you have set yourself.

Apart from the necessity to tailor your premises policy to suit your business objectives, the strategies to be considered also depend on the nature of the underlying problems that have brought your premises to the forefront as a growth problem. For instance, shortage of space, too much space, inefficient use of space, inadequate internal environment, image, location, corporate centralization, corporate decentralization, flexibility, premises costs, staff costs, redundancy policy, real estate factors, accountancy policy, comments from your customers, suppliers or bank manager and so on. Each of these problems or complaints suggests its own remedy.

Although each problem may suggest a different solution, however, most businesses have a choice of several main options such as stay and make alterations as necessary, move away to new location(s) or some combination of these options. The option of staying and altering the premises probably means effecting some compromise. The extent and quality of the alterations together with any tenure factors will decide the economics of this option. Sometimes, in the case of over-supply of space, part of the existing premises may be prepared for leasing or sub-leasing. Apart from the effect on premises, the costs of remaining in your present premises or moving to a new location will also have to take into account the cost of staff, turnover of staff, availability of staff, travel times to, from and during work, plus less substantial but important factors such as image.

There are many ways of looking at the costs of a premises strategy and for comparing one with another. These range from fairly simple 'annual premises costs' calculations to highly sophisticated techniques of cost benefit analysis. The annual costs method – which involves you in identifying the key areas of cost (rent, maintenance, cleaning, transport, production space, communications and administration, etc.) and calculating the current costs for each of these 'cost centres' – is a useful preliminary analysis, because it allows you to make quick comparisons, with your own costs at different periods of time. By weighting each of the cost centres according to its importance to you or your business, you can add them together to produce a weighted 'score'.

This 'weighted evaluation' technique enables you to evaluate each of your options according to your own criteria and enables you to make quick comparisons between alternative premises. The total points score gives a reasonably sensible view of how you see the options in performance terms. More sophisticated techniques, such as life-cycle cost analysis, normally require the skills of a professional surveyor or building economist who has to try to forecast such things as the extent of rent reviews, the changes in rates, premiums on leases surrendered, re-active and pro-active maintenance service charges, operating costs, fitting out costs and inflation.

Lease or buy?

If you do decide that some new premises are in order, you are then faced with the familiar question of whether to lease or buy. Of course, if your growth has left your cash reserves rather low you will need to postpone that decision unless you find a new injection of finance (see next chapter). However, apart from the financial considerations, there are also the legal constraints (covered in *The Barclays Guide to Law for the Small Business*) to take into account. For instance, the effect of making radical and expensive alterations to a leasehold property – for example, upgrading for computers or other information technology – must be carefully considered within the terms of the lease. Also, you will need to take into account the legal obligations and costs likely to be incurred as either a landlord (if you are planning to buy new premises and then let part of them) or a tenant (if you intend to occupy rented premises). You should also make sure, if you do not already know, what your legal rights are as a landlord or tenant, because you may find that you do not have quite the freedom of action (or the obligations) that you originally thought you had. (*The Barclays Guide to Law for the Small Business* also covers the rights and duties of landlords and tenants, though often they depend on the actual terms of your lease or contract.) For instance, it is not at all unusual for tenants to have their rents revised to a level reflecting the improvements they have paid for themselves.

If you are a tenant you need not be too concerned about the ratio of net internal to gross internal floor area. Rent is paid on the net internal area. However, common services such as heating, air conditioning, window cleaning, maintenance and upkeep are all related to the gross amount of space and building volume, with the result that operating costs are sensitive to uneconomical gross building design. Developers, however, have the most to lose from not getting the maximum lettable (net internal) floor space out of the gross area, and work hard to achieve efficient gross to net ratios – sometimes at the expense of lettable to usable ratios, which are the prime concern of the final user. In this regard, there can be advantages in getting into a development early enough (either as a tenant or owner) to have the building tailored to suit your requirements – often without a cost penalty.

At this point, it is worth mentioning that as your decisions regarding your premises may involve very large sums of money and longer-term obligations, which may not be immediately apparent, it would be wise, if the move is a major one, to consult professional advisers – not only your accountant but also a solicitor and, equally importantly, a qualified surveyor (who usually know a lot more about buildings than just their structural defects). Remember at all times, however, when dealing with professional advisers that you are paying their fees and that you have every right to expect them to answer your questions to your satisfaction not theirs!

Having consulted your advisers, you may find that it is far better to do a deal with the landlord and sign a new agreement whereby some or all of the costs (such as maintenance, refurbishment, decoration, fitting out, etc.) are included in a slightly increased rent. This will normally be a better bet than directly funding these costs yourself out of cash flow or on a commercial mortgage, even though you will, of course, have normal reviews on the extra rent in the 'rentalized' option. Indeed, if your business is expanding rapidly, your premises needs could also change rapidly over the next few years and you do not want to find yourself locked into unsuitable premises. Property can be deceptively easy to buy (on borrowed money) but awkwardly difficult to sell if you need to boost your liquidity suddenly.

Consequently, even though there is sometimes a temptation to buy property on the grounds that it will steadily improve your balance sheet as it increases in value, it is more important to think about your present and future profit and loss and cash flow positions before committing yourself to purchasing property. Remember that your premises policy should match your business plan. Unless yours is a property development or investment company you should think of your premises as plant to aid your business. Do not ignore the real estate implications but equally, do not let them dictate the decision. Indeed, even if you do decide to purchase, you should employ the same approach in deciding whether it would be wiser to buy freehold or opt for a leasehold. Although your final decision may be determined by such considerations as availability, accountancy, financial status, flexibility, image, location or, probably, a combination of all or some of these factors, you should also take into account your longer-term plans for the business as well as the shorter-term need to manage cash flow.

Summary

This chapter has examined the effects of growth on your existing premises and outlined the steps that you need to take in analysing your next move. The main options of remaining but redesigning and refurbishing your existing premises to meet your future needs or relocating to new premises were analysed. The basic areas of information upon which you could make sensible decisions were identified and discussed.

Key points

- Measure your actual, usable work area.
- Assess how much space members of staff need to ensure the efficient running of your business.
- Estimate your future premises needs on the likely future size of your workforce.
- Taking into account the financial implications and your business image and future growth plans, decide whether to refurbish or relocate.
- If you decide to move, consider the full legal and financial implications in deciding whether to lease or buy.

6

Keeping your finances under control

Outline

If your growth is heading out of control, you will quickly realize that fact when your business starts to go off the tracks financially. Fortunately, if you take the trouble to look, your financial records will contain enough early signals to warn you in time. This chapter outlines how you can:

- keep a proper track of your finances
- make use of financial information to monitor your business
- avoid the pitfalls of overtrading
- speed up payments from your debtors
- finance the next stage of your growth

This next major area, that of financial control, is essential to your planning process. But, even before financial control is addressed, you must ensure that your financial records are accurate, sufficient and easily understood. The financial aspects of growth and good business 'house-keeping' are fully examined in *The Barclays Guide to Financial Management for the Small Business*. This chapter explores the organizational and management implications of these issues and emphasizes the importance of invoicing, debtor control and cash-flow management to expanding businesses.

After dealing with the necessity of keeping and using clear financial records and procedures, this chapter explains some of the more useful yet sophisticated financial ratios. Finally, the question of finance for future growth is tackled with some hints on types of finance available and warnings of the dangers of undercapitalization.

Keeping track of your finances

Businesses must make profits to grow successfully, and if you find yourself growing but not making any real profits (or, even worse, actually losing money), then you are staring business failure in the face. This will be particularly so if you find that your cash is even slower to come in than your paper profits. In the short term, new firms and growing firms need cash to meet their obligations and, if growth is rapid and unexpected, there is a very real danger that lack of cash can drive you out of business. Indeed, as pointed out in *The Barclays Guide to Law for the Small Business*, you may be risking more than a failed business, because, company or no, you may be trading outside the protection of your limited liability if you continue to trade when you are making a loss (sometimes, whether or not you are actually aware of the situation). Therefore, during your survival or rapid growth period, monitoring the cash flow into and out of the business is vital.

Make it a top priority that your financial records are well kept and in order. Once you are sure that your recording systems are accurate and that you are effectively organized to deal with this sort of information (see chapter 4), you are in a position to begin to monitor the actual performance of your business. To ensure continued growth you must monitor the two major variables that affect profit and that you can control – margins and overheads. Your *margins* – or gross profits – represent the difference between your revenue from sales and the direct costs of those sales (materials, wages, transport, etc.) while your *overheads* are the indirect costs that you incur in keeping your business running (administration, rent, maintenance, etc.). Because some of these direct and indirect costs will remain much the same for a given output of goods or services (e.g., rent, equipment, office costs, etc.) but others – being linked to your volume of output of goods or services (e.g., power, lighting, raw materials, part-time labour, etc.) – will vary, your margins will fluctuate as your sales rise or fall. To complicate matters further, your 'fixed' costs are also likely to change if your output goes above or below certain levels, and the rate of increase in the 'variable' costs may go either up or down as output increases.

Clearly, there is a relationship between sales and gross profits, and between gross profits, overheads and your eventual net profits. Equally clearly, merely monitoring sales will not alert you to any potentially disastrous drop in margins or increase in overheads – particularly if they are changing faster than your increase in sales revenue. However, it can take some time to collect the right information to calculate your profits and precise changes to overheads or margins, so it is best to have some idea of how margins and overheads relate to sales, and to monitor these broader relationships. If you express margins and total overheads as a percentage of sales, you can compare the actual figures each month (or each quarter or each week, depending on which period is most suitable for you) with the figures that you budgeted for, based on past experience and your present expectations. Identifying the common growth problem of rising sales but falling profits as either due to falling margins or rising overheads will also help in identifying the solution to the problem. These terms and techniques are fully explained in *The Barclays Guide to Financial Management for the Small Business*.

To illustrate these important points further, take our two fictitious firms – Batchjob and Compburo. It is easy to see the security offered to Batchjob by regular, jobbing sub-contracts, if regular, standard invoices mean a reliable flow of payments with no requirement to outlay money on new machines. The higher-risk (and higher value-added) alternative of seeking more customized, small-batch contracts may involve additional investment and increased labour costs (all of which would have to be paid for immediately) and may result in delays in invoicing and receiving payments for each one-off job. With Compburo, the situation may be the reverse but equally disastrous. Clients may be slow to pay for contracts completed in Compburo's studio while bigger clients, hungry for trained technical skills in their own operations, may be prepared to agree terms of payment that include fees in advance (but payment to freelance staff in arrears). Although dealing with slower payers of larger sums of money, the studio-based contracts would still have to cover studio staff wages and leasing or hire-purchase payments on expensive CAD (computer assisted design) machines. In either case, it is not too difficult to see that excessive growth in the areas which present payment problems could soon lead to a severe cash shortage. Staff, equipment suppliers, VAT inspectors and many other creditors tend to create enormous problems if they fail to get paid on time.

Thus, you need to monitor cash flow and your profit margins very carefully and, if you are growing, you need to be especially vigilant. For instance, if your gross profits from sales appear to have fallen, make sure that you check whether it is because your sales volumes are down or because your costs of sales have risen. If it is the latter, try to identify whether the rise in costs is due to the effects of inflation on the wholesale prices of your supplies or to an increase in your overhead costs (energy, staff, rent, equipment hire, materials wastage rates, and so on). The margin has been reduced and unless some way to restore it (by changing suppliers, managing the use of energy and materials more effectively, minimizing the use of high-cost labour on each job, and so on) can be found, the business will not meet its target. If costs are unlikely to come back to previous levels, then decisions on prices and their likely effects on volumes (this holds true for both manufacturers and service businesses) will have to be taken.

Indeed, the monitoring of costs is fundamental to the process of managing and should be conducted on a fairly frequent and regular basis. In most businesses there is far too much activity going on for it all to be monitored economically, and there is small point in monitoring something which has little effect on your business. However, most businesses face promotional and operating costs. In all cases if a cost is significant, either directly or indirectly, it must be monitored. Also, another key area to monitor is the effectiveness of your sales. Because all businesses are different, how you monitor the sale or promotion of your own goods and services will not be exactly the same as the methods appropriate for many other businesses. In general, however, there are a few key questions that you need answered. In relation to direct sales promotion you need to find out how effective were the advertising, publicity, displays, special events, promotions and so on. You will also need to know the relative costs of each with respect to sales revenue. It would also be helpful for future promotional activity to be able to identify which newspapers, magazines and periodicals yielded the best sales in relation to their advertising rates. The same questions arise about indirect sales promotion. You need to have some idea about how useful it is for your business to spend money on public relations, customer relations, customer services, packaging, logos and so on.

Finally, a few words on the actual process of monitoring. If you are concerned about keeping control of your costs and measuring changes in performance, you need to collect and scan relevant information on a regular basis. You also need to identify, even if just by trial and error, the ratios or figures that pick up the changes you are interested in keeping an eye on and that are fairly straightforward for you to use. And last but not least, the whole notion of monitoring implies that you have some standards against which you are judging any shifts (past performance, expected performance, average previous costs, projected costs and so on). This in turn implies that you will have produced some form of budget, with your performance, costs and revenue targets clearly stated, and that your monitoring consists of identifying any significant variations from budget figures in key areas. What these key areas are will, of course, depend on what is relevant to your business performance. For instance, petty cash should not be a significant item in your business and you could stand quite a large variation, say 15–20 per cent, in minor items of expenditure (coffee money, postage, and so on). However, if you run a mail-order business, a surveying consultancy or any other business that makes fairly extensive use of couriers or postal services, then delivery costs could account for a significant proportion of your costs, which you need to monitor rather tightly. In this case, a variation of even 5 per cent may be significant.

The basic documentation and records that you need to keep have already been mentioned on pp. 26–7 on the processes involved in controlling growth. Also, how your business should be re-structured so that this type of information reaches you and can be quickly acted upon was examined on pp. 46–50 which dealt with how to structure your organization for growth. However, growing businesses need to step beyond the basic accounts level. With growth, you begin to encounter many more business problems that involve making decisions. For instance, faced with different profiles of product profitability and future market-growth prospects, you have to decide upon which product or service to concentrate your selling efforts. Having decided that issue (but only for the time being, not for when the market changes in, say, six months' time), you then have to decide which precise market to aim for, how best to reach that market and at what pricing level.

Faced with several options you need some way to assess which gives you the best return for the investment you have made. Indeed, this type of decision becomes imperative if you responded to growth by raising finance to invest in your growth areas (see pp. 97–103). *The Barclays Guide to Financial Management for the Small Business* explains and contrasts a number of commonly used accounting measures that bankers, accountants, investors and dynamic managers of growing businesses tend to use for deciding between a number of competing options for management and investment time. For instance, one commonly used measure, though not necessarily the most appropriate for your purposes, is *return on capital employed* (ROCE). Very crudely, if Batchjob's regular sub-contracts make annual profits of £100,000 for an investment of £50,000 while small-batch contracts require a larger investment of £80,000 but yield profits of £200,000, the option offering the highest return on capital employed is the small-batch contracts with a ROCE of 2.5 times (200,000/80,000) compared with the regular jobbing contracts a return of just two times (100,000/50,000). Therefore, if Batchjob's owner can speed up the payments for the customized small-batch jobs and minimize the lags in the cash flow for those types of contracts (see p. 93), he seems to be right in redirecting his energies towards more small-batch contracts.

The use of financial information to control the progress of your business extends further than just calculating your return on capital. For instance, in Batchjob and Compburo – although their strategies are rather different – it seems plain that, in both cases, they are not facing a simple choice between two options. Instead, the wisest course for both businesses is to go for a mixed strategy of guaranteeing cash flow through one type of contract and boosting overall ROCE through the other type of contract. In other words, both businesses should be going for their own unique mix of options (these questions of strategy are developed further in chapter 8). Apart from ROCE, which can also be used as a tool for analysing future investment, performance in particular areas of your business can be controlled through a variety of ratios, such as liquidity ratios for measuring your ability to pay your creditors, ratios to monitor your effectiveness in the use of resources, or profitability ratios for judging your success at generating profits.

Most businesses only make use of a few key ratios and you should discuss with your accountant which ones, apart from ROCE (they are explained in detail in *The Barclays Guide to Financial Manage-*

ment for the Small Business), you should be monitoring. Ultimately, you will need to determine your own ROCE targets, taking into account your present business, future trends, your own objectives and your intended growth plans. Remember that from the moment you began trading, cash flow, profitability, working capital and fixed-asset management became key areas to monitor (even if you were not aware of it at the time), and they become even more important to control as you grow and set new ROCE targets.

Using financial information

You do not have to be a trained accountant to be able to make effective use of the financial information that you collect for your own planning purposes. Indeed, you may not have time to discuss events with your accountant. If you are growing fast in a changing world, you need to be able to react quickly to avoid sudden dangers and to take advantage of temporary opportunities. The key to effective use of financial information lies in knowing what part of your business performance you want to monitor, what yardsticks (financial or otherwise) you need for effectively monitoring that performance, and how to judge the significance of any changes. To maintain growth, new ROCE targets will need to be set, and a new cycle of identifying areas of your business that can increase sales and profits, while decreasing costs, commences again. You will be looking to reduce working capital, increase stock turnover, speed up customer payment, promote working efficiency, develop a more streamlined organization, as well as many other things already mentioned in this book.

Once again, these imply that you have a clear idea of your objectives, and that you have managed to write down your expectations for your business so that you can instantly see if you are going off-course or growing faster than you anticipated. As mentioned above, actual performance is monitored against budgets, so that when events go wrong corrective action can be taken. To gain full value from the monitoring process, you need to be sure of measurement criteria and you need to know where you are going and why. Planning is essential to control any activity – it is the way aims, objectives and targets are set. It is a two-way process between the top and bottom, out of which budget targets can emerge, which reflect the growth of your business, and which your staff feel are attainable and a sound basis upon which to judge their performance. However, the monitoring system must provide information quickly, clearly and in just the right amount of detail for you to be able to use it. Too much information and you will be swamped – too little and you run the risk of being ill prepared. Without planning and budgetary control you have little chance of success.

Planning can be viewed simply as putting on paper the aims and purposes of the organization, and the targets which it intends to achieve within the time period (usually one year, but it can be more or less, depending on your situation). Typical targets that firms set for their products in each of the various markets in which they trade can be expressed in terms of sales volume, market share, profit, return on capital and a number of other criteria. These issues will be discussed again more fully in chapters 8 and 9.

Avoiding the pitfalls of overtrading

Expansion brings many dangers to the firm. All too often, profitable, expanding companies go bankrupt simply because their additional sales carry increased costs and the extra costs of growth force them to run out of cash. As mentioned in chapter 1, this danger is called *overtrading*, and, often, the owner-managers of the failed businesses did not realize that they were overtrading because they failed to monitor the accounting information that would have informed them it was happening. Expanding firms can need considerable investments of cash to finance extra staff, increased storage, higher volumes of supplies and inputs and, sometimes, new machines. Indeed, if you suddenly land a large and unexpected order, be on guard. Many a business owner has been blinded by the prospect of instant growth and did not see that all sales have a cost and that frequently the costs have to be paid before the income from the sales is in hand. Even if you are making a profit on paper, you still need cash to pay your staff's wages and – unless you can arrange favourable credit terms – for your increasing supplies as well. In some service businesses, the hidden costs may be even more severe, because services often rely on skilled staff, and a sudden large contract is likely to mean an increase in such staff.

If your business is new or growing rapidly, as was mentioned in a previous section, it is unlikely that you will be able to generate sufficient cash from your operations to cover your new and increasing costs. If you are serious about growth, you will need to turn to other sources of additional finance such as private investors, bankers or venture capitalists. The issues involved in raising growth finance are discussed in the next section. The important point here is that these sources of finance are primarily interested in the financial performance of your business. It is, therefore, vital that you monitor key financial variables closely (as outlined in the previous section), often on a daily basis, but at least on a weekly basis. You must decide what are the key financial variables that need close scrutiny for your business. Sales always need to be monitored closely but, to avoid falling into the trap of overtrading, your cash-flow budget is your vital tool.

Keeping on top of your cash flow is necessary because money is continually moving into and out of a business and it can be difficult to keep track of. However, it is vital that you do so because, at the end of the day, the bills are paid with cash not with profit. As we have seen in a previous section, our fictitious examples Batchjob and Compburo both faced running out of cash on one of their products because of slow payments. Businesses can be profitable but still run out of cash and you need cash to survive. If you cannot survive, the future is unimportant, no matter how rosy the profit forecasts might be. Highly profitable opportunities may present themselves, but they can result in a company running out of that vital ingredient – cash.

Of course, it may be possible to borrow the cash needed, if you plan ahead, but either way a cash-flow forecast is essential. The cash-flow forecast involves making estimates of all cash receipts and cash expenditures. This means that you have to estimate what you might sell, at what price and when you expect to receive the cash from these sales. It also means that you have to estimate the costs you would incur in achieving those sales and when you would pay the bills. The cash-flow forecast should enable you to calculate the cash surplus or deficit for the months ahead. If these figures are added to the monthly estimated opening cash balance, the estimated closing balance for the month can be calculated.

The important thing about any cash-flow forecast is to learn from it in order to give early warning to yourself or the bank of additional financing requirements. If there are serious discrepancies between budgeted and actual figures (for example, there may be an un-expected need to replace an expensive item of equipment – a precision lathe for Batchjob or a CAD machine for Compburo) then the cash flow needs to be replanned. Although the budgeting process is complex and estimates are difficult to make, there are some tech-niques that can help you. It is sometimes helpful to visualize the process as a circular waterpipe with various inflow and outflow taps (see Exhibit 6.1). The water, which represents cash, enters the system from a regulatory cistern which can accommodate more water but which must never run dry if the system is to survive. The outflow taps, which let water escape from the pipe, represent payments on working capital (the money that you consume in the day-to-day working of your business), creditors and stocks (raw materials, work-in-progress, finished goods), while the inflow taps, which let more water into the pipe, represent debtors and cash customers. The pipe starts and ends in the cistern but its purpose is to turn the original volume of water (cash) into a larger volume. However, the water is continually gurgling around the system and it is not always easy to see exactly what is happening.

Obviously, the size and routeing of the pipe, the plumbing in the system, the efficiency of the tap valves and the points where the inflow and outflow taps are located vary for different sorts of business (manufacturing, retail, service, transport, construction, etc.). But it is clear that the volume of inflow has to exceed the volume of outflow if the cistern is not to run dry eventually. It should also be clear that, if the inflow is bigger than the outflow, the cistern will fill more quickly if the flow of water is faster. The flow can be speeded up, by ensuring faster and sizeable inflows and by reducing outflows. Leaving the hydraulic world of water pipes, the flow of cash through your business can be speeded up by, for instance, collecting debts more quickly, taking more credit from creditors, holding minimum stocks and adopting new cost-saving measures. On the other hand, cash flow can be slowed down by offering extended credit to cus-tomers, paying creditors more quickly or holding more stocks. In general, expansion of your business will have the effect of slowing down the cash-flow cycle.

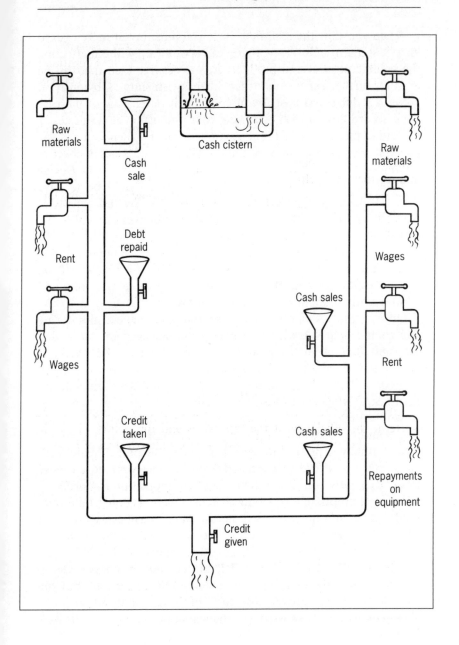

Exhibit 6.1 Cash-flow cycle

When you slow the cash-flow cycle you must invest more cash to keep it spinning. However, if you can speed it up without affecting the volume of sales and production, you set free cash that can be used for further expansion (or for other investments). Obviously, if you can reduce your costs by more prudent purchasing or increase your inward flow of cash by raising your proportion of cash sales or by selling more to your faster-paying customers, then you can say that you are managing your cash flow efficiently (the issues of effective buying and selling are covered in *The Barclays Guide to Buying and Selling for the Small Business*). Your aim should be to have your business wheel of fortune running as smoothly and quickly as possible, and clearly the clue to your successful management of the cash-flow cycle lies in having effective systems of debtor and credit control, plus an efficient method of stock control. In organizational terms, this returns us to the issues discussed on pp. 46–50 on how to restructure your business – especially your central office and administrative functions – to deal with growth.

Once again, this highlights the importance of financial monitoring and should help you identify some of the management ratios that you will find useful in monitoring your business effectively. If your aim is to reduce your stock and debtor turnovers to a minimum number of days (which will vary from district to district and industry to industry) while lengthening your creditor turnover to as many days as you can manage without impairing your reputation, you should find liquidity ratios and average creditor, debtor and stock turnover ratios (usually expressed in days) particularly helpful. Usually with stock you can afford to concentrate on keeping your dozen or so most frequently consumed items regularly topped up (by ordering them in appropriately economic batches) while keeping minimum holdings of infrequently used items. Many businesses find that roughly 80 per cent of their stock turnover is accounted for by around 20 per cent of stock items (other aspects of this 80:20 rule are discussed in chapter 7), and it makes good business sense to ensure that you do not run out of the important 20 per cent, but you can afford to keep relatively low stocks of the remaining 80 per cent – slow-moving items (or whatever the actual percentages are in your business).

Debtor control starts with making sure that every order clearly carries your terms of sale which should include as many cash sales as possible, and no more than thirty days' credit for your non-cash sales (unless there are established credit periods in your industry). If you have reorganized your office system, it should be your established practice by now either to send pro forma invoices before delivery of your goods or services or to invoice as promptly as you can and to send a reminder invoice automatically (with suitable apologies if payment has crossed in the post) to all overdue accounts as they fall overdue. The next stage can involve a follow-up letter reminding customers of the terms of credit and insisting on the payment of interest if the payment of the debt is further delayed. If the sums are reasonably large you could then consider legal action. Of course, if you do receive a large order from a new client, make sure that you obtain references on the client before extending credit, and approach your bank or a specialized agency to run a credit check. If you are growing quickly, it is vital to keep your debtor turnover under control but, especially if credit is the norm in your industry, you may find it hard to ensure that your cash is coming in as fast as you would like. If you are in this situation, you may begin to feel the need for extra finance to cover not only shortfalls in your cash position but also the new staff and equipment that you need to sustain your growth.

Financing your growth

Raising money is rarely an easy undertaking. You first need to determine how much you need and when you need it. You then need to decide what finance is appropriate for your firm. Following these steps will help you to save time, avoid undue expense, and improve your chances of raising the finance you need. Bear in mind that most small businesses seek their extra financing from banks, and a low return on capital employed (ROCE) will make it difficult to attract new funds to finance growth and will limit your growth prospects. However, you can only determine the finance you need accurately by proper financial budgeting. In particular, the cash-flow forecast should show you any shortfall in your cash requirements. It should show you how much you need, and when you need it. *The Barclays Guide to Financial Management for the Small Business* will help you with the skills you need to draw up a complete set of budgets including not only cash-flow forecasts but also profit and loss forecasts and balance sheet forecasts.

If you have not already prepared these budgets, you will have to do so at some stage. Most small firms finance the bulk of their expansion plans from funds generated by the business itself. The problem with this is that you may have to wait a long time before you have sufficient funds. On the other hand, you may be able to speed up the generation of these funds, or indeed minimize the capital you need for expansion, by more efficient management of your working capital. As mentioned above, you should start by looking at how efficient you are at controlling your debtors or stock, not only to improve your cash flow but also to impress any potential source of finance with how well you manage your business. Once you know how much you need and when you need it, you must decide on what form that money should take.

Finding the appropriate funds to finance the growth of your business is important. If you fail to find the right amount or even the right form of finance, it could lead to bankruptcy or loss of control of your business. Different forms of finance have to be bought at a price, and according to their own terms and conditions. It may be time-consuming, but it usually does pay you to shop around to get the best price and conditions. Indeed, if you are tied to only one supplier, you face the risk that the source might dry up. So, as you grow, you should develop a diversified range of funding from different sources. A company that is adequately and safely funded faces a far better chance of growing successfully and weathering the inevitable storms.

To make sure that you do approach your quest for extra finance in the right frame of mind, you should ask yourself a number of questions. Perhaps the most basic question – indeed the fundamental purpose of your acquiring this book – is whether you can identify strong and specific evidence that you can expand. After you have satisfied yourself that there are solid grounds for your belief that you can continue to grow, you have to decide how much finance you need to support your intended growth. Once again, you should also be sure in your own mind that you can justify the amount of finance you say that you need. In practice, this means that you should identify and list all the items that you need to spend money on (machines, premises, other equipment, staff, supplies, and so on), and estimate their cost. You will also need to outline the time scale over which you expect to spend the money. Before consulting your accountant or committing yourself, try to read the relevant sections in *The Barclays Guide to Financial Management for the Small Business.*

The next question to consider is the form that you feel this finance could take (short-term loan, longer-term investment, extra share capital, and so on). Although the basic form of any loan is quite clear – an agreed amount is lent to the borrower for an agreed period of time, to be repaid in a number of instalments often spread evenly over the repayment period – there are a number of different types of loans and various costs associated with them. An arrangement fee is normally charged to cover the legal and administrative costs involved in arranging the loan, but you have to make sure that any arrangement fee is reasonable and not excessive. Arrangement fees usually take the form of either a fixed fee or a percentage of the loan.

The most obvious cost of any loan is, of course, the rate of interest which is charged as a percentage rate applied to the amount of the loan outstanding. The interest rate can be *fixed* for the period of the loan, or it can be *variable*, in that it is linked to the bank discount or base rate (which can fluctuate). Of course, the rate is determined by a number of economic factors such as general money market rates and the money supply, as well as intervention by the Bank of England. This means that variable rates are liable to vary during the course of a loan (which is either good or bad depending on the pressures on the banks' base rate). Some business owners find it easier to plan ahead if they are dealing with a fixed interest rate (although it is obviously wiser to avoid fixed rates if you believe that interest rates are due to fall). All arrangement fees and interest rates are negotiable and, in some under-developed regions, it is possible to find *soft loans*, which have rates of interest below base rate, or even a 'capital holiday', which means that there is no repayment of the loan during that period. Similarly a 'rest period' means a delay (normally no more than two years) before you start paying interest as well as repaying capital.

The terms and conditions of loans are written in legal documents known as *debentures*. The more typical conditions attached to loans by lenders are outlined below but the full legal implications are explained in *The Barclays Guide to Law for the Small Business*. Loans from banks and most other common sources of finance are *secured*, which means that the lender is entitled, under certain conditions, to some of your assets as protection, should you not be able to keep to the terms and conditions of the debenture. That security can be a *fixed charge* on specific assets in the business or the loan can be secured against property as a *mortgage*. The security can also be on all or any of the business assets as a *floating charge*. Lenders may also ask for personal guarantees, which means that the lender has recourse to your personal assets if the business is unable to repay a loan.

Obviously, offering personal guarantees or other extra conditions – such as the stipulation that no further loans can be taken out by your business without the approval of the lender until the present loan is repaid or the specified performance of certain minimum financial ratios – are to be resisted. Also, take note that the lender has no entitlement to any management or control of the business. Lenders' rights are set out in the debenture document and they cannot go beyond those terms and conditions to interfere in your business. However, you do need to take care that you do not breach those conditions – by, for example, defaulting on repayments – because the lenders may then have the power to have your company wound up. If these costs and conditions seem over-onerous, however, you could consider offering investors an opportunity to invest directly in your business.

To be able to attract direct investment, your business has to be set up as an incorporated partnership or an incorporated limited liability company. Partnerships can increase their number of partners, but the new partners may find that their liability extends beyond the amount they have invested in the partnership. Consequently, the most common legal form that can offer shares in exchange for external finance (provided its articles of association allow for such an arrangement) is the limited liability company. Indeed, if you are now seeking substantial amounts of finance for growth, it is generally easier and more prudent to do so as a limited liability company, unless you face certain tax and reporting disadvantages or other reasons why you should not do so. However, any proposed change in your business's legal status may have legal and tax implications involving, for example, share valuation or contractual matters and you would be well advised, before seeking professional advice, to read *The Barclays Guide to Law for the Small Business*.

There are a number of sources of direct investment, ranging from individual private investors through Business Expansion Scheme funds or venture capital funds on to private placements, investments by prospectus and, eventually, the stock exchange (either as a full listing or on the unlisted securities market). This form of direct investment is usually referred to as *equity* funding because the investors also acquire rights to dividends and to vote. It is this right to vote on how the business is managed that often discourages small business owners from seeking equity finance, even though there is no legal obligation to make regular payments, especially if the business is not making a profit. With most private investors, however, the legal rights of the shareholder need not prove to be too much of a hurdle, because the share could be confined to well under half the equity (or under one quarter if you want to retain the absolute right to sell the company or put it into liquidation).

Unfortunately, there are now relatively few such direct private investors because most sources of equity finance come from venture capitalists or special funds, and these frequently want equity stakes of 40 per cent or more. In addition, these professional investors can insist on being given preferential treatment as part of the conditions of investment and, even before they invest one penny, they frequently insist on borrowers producing sheaves of time-consuming proposals, records, accounts and even prospectuses. Normally, these preparation costs far exceed any arrangement fees that you may be required to pay for a loan. Provided you are not trying to raise money from a stock market, however, raising equity finance should be less of a burden on your early cash flow than raising loan finance.

Of course, there are both advantages and disadvantages in opting either for loans or for shares. When you take out a loan you do not give away ownership or control of the business. The lender cannot interfere in the way you choose to run your business. If the business prospers, you stand to gain, not the lender. On the other hand, the lender must be paid interest regularly and the capital repayments must also be met, as laid down in the debenture document. Even if the business is not doing very well, these payments must still be made, otherwise the lender may wind up the company and seize certain assets. If you have given personal guarantees, you may have to meet any shortfall yourself. Loans allow you to keep control, but interest and capital repayments must be met.

When you issue ordinary shares to other people, you give away part of the company. You lose total ownership and some control, but you do improve your chances of securing more finance in the future. Furthermore, especially if your shareholders do not immediately expect their share of the company's profits, in the form of dividends, raising funds through share issues – equity capital – can be cheaper and impose less of a cash flow drain on your company. In fact, dividends need only be paid when the directors decide to do so. If the majority of shareholders recognize that the business is not doing well, dividends need not be paid. If, on the other hand, the business is doing rather well and dividends are paid, it still may be more advantageous and thrifty to issue share capital (which you can do up to a certain limit without losing control). Lenders expect a certain relationship, referred to as *gearing* or *leverage*, between the amount of share capital and the amount of loan capital. With more share capital, your proportion of total capital represented by loans will not seem so high. Consequently when you issue shares, you will probably improve the ability of the company to take out further loans. You may give away your complete ownership of your company with shares, but you increase your borrowing capacity.

Many foreign banks are apparently now happy to provide equity capital rather than loan capital. Indeed, as the Single Market becomes more evident, new sources of finance should appear. However, you should always seek professional advice when dealing with finance, because many of these new sources of finance offer interesting mixes of equity and loan finance, especially for management buy-outs and acquisitions. For instance, *preference shares* – those that are paid out at a fixed rate before the ordinary investors are paid their dividends – have characteristics of both loans and shares. If they are redeemable then you should not lose ownership of the company, although you will have to find the capital repayment. You will only lose control if you fall behind on the dividend payments. If they are convertible, then you may lose both ownership and control of the company at some future date. On the other hand, if the shares are cumulative, the fixed dividends will always have to be met, whether or not the company is profitable. What is more, this dividend comes out of after-tax income.

Thus, there are a number of courses to steer between loan and share capital when you are seeking finance to fund your growth.

What you should hope to achieve is some form of balance between loan and share capital. Once you are satisfied that you have identified the financial balance that is appropriate for your business in its current situation, you have then to decide on the most suitable source of your finance. In part, this will be determined by the type of finance that you favour. However, financial services are an inventive industry and there are plenty of new sources. Your accountant, your bank manager and *The Barclays Guide to Financial Management for the Small Business* should all help you choose the right path for financing your future growth.

Summary

This chapter has addressed the important issue that separates unplanned businesses from those that adopt a more structured approach to their growth – the efficient management of your finances. Starting from the need to keep accurate financial records, this chapter outlined how you can make use of financial information to provide yourself with helpful management information and how to plan for your future financial needs as your business continues to grow.

Key points

- Keep accurate and useful financial records.
- Identify which financial budgets and monitoring ratios are suitable for your business.
- Use appropriate financial information to monitor your business performance and cash flow.
- Use financial ratios to monitor your creditor, debtor and stock turnovers.
- Make use of your existing financial information to predict your future financial needs.
- Select the right mix of equity and loan finance to fund your future growth.

7

Focusing on your growth products

Outline

This chapter deals with the main management issues associated with the need to decide simple strategies for analysing your most profitable products and your best target customers. In addition, this chapter draws your attention to the need to develop new products and how to introduce them as painlessly as possible. Techniques for researching markets and identifying future growth areas are also discussed. In this chapter we consider:

- targeting growth customers
- researching markets and trends
- managing weak products
- developing new products

Having addressed the more physical problems of growth – staffing and premises – you are now in a position to turn your attention to some of the more analytical problems which lie at the heart of business planning. The first of these is the need to make sure that your business efforts are concentrated on the right products and the appropriate customers. If you stay stuck on a low-profit or unprofitable product, your growth problems may just be early warning signals of an imminent bankruptcy.

The main marketing issues raised in this chapter are covered more fully in *The Barclays Guide to Marketing for the Small Business*.

Targeting growth customers

Just as products can be seen as moving through a life cycle (described on p. 25 ff.) – from birth, through growth, maturity and consolidation

104

and (in the absence of any adjustments to the basic product) into an inevitable decline – the development of businesses can be described in similar terms. There is, of course, no guarantee that your business will, in fact, move up the growth curve (shown on p. 23) without succumbing to one of the major crises that lie on its path. Apart from the financial and organizational considerations that you have to take into account, your chances of overcoming the business-growth crisis points depend greatly on your ability to be able to identify correctly your target customers and constantly to make sure that your products do satisfy their needs. Few small businesses start out with such a *customer-oriented* approach and it is not surprising that many eventually fail. This is particularly true of many smaller firms that depend – perhaps exclusively – on one major product. It is by no means unusual for businesses to start by producing one major good item or providing one type of service, and then, if their product satisfies customer wants, to begin to grow. Unfortunately, very few small businesses realize the dangers of remaining tied to the fate of a single product (even if it is initially extremely successful) or the more deeply-rooted problems that flow from being too product-oriented.

Question 14 How many goods or services do you currently offer? Can you define them in terms of main customer segments? Are any of your products showing signs of wear in terms of declining sales or profit margins?

Basically, there are two marketing challenges that growth – whether planned or unplanned – throws up. The first, which is discussed in this section, is the need to make the switch from being product-oriented to being customer-oriented. In fact, as your answer to question 8 on p. 25 may have indicated, one of the main under-pinnings in any successful growth strategy is the constant need to take into account your target customers. The second challenge, which is discussed below on pp. 117–122, is the need to keep on developing new products and new markets as the sales of existing products begin to consolidate. This means, of course, that the need to keep aware of trends and developments in your main markets is paramount (and a major reason why you need to free yourself from routine or low-priority tasks as discussed in chapter 3). The main techniques for keeping abreast with what is going on are covered in the next section as are the principal methods used for identifying your most important types of customers and monitoring their behaviour – a task of crucial importance.

For instance, if Batchjob – our fictitious small engineering firm – relied solely on producing particular components or sub-assemblies for one dominant client, their fortunes as a business would depend almost entirely on continued customer demand for the completed product produced by their client. Consequently, even assuming that there are no changes to the client's design of the product and that their client remains well managed and is not affected by competition (locally, nationally or, as a result of the Single Market, in Europe), a shift in customer demand or the arrival of more advanced substitute products in the market could easily lead – indeed, should inevitably lead – to a decline in sales of the product and a decline in Batchjob's fortunes. This is another sound reason for Batchjob's owner to pursue his preferred strategy of seeking higher value-added small-batch contracts from a variety of clients rather than rely on supposedly steady, longer-term, higher-volume jobbing contracts from one or a few main clients.

Similarly, if Compburo started by successfully providing a computer-based design service to outside clients, but did not notice that more and more people were being trained in the specialist skills that they themselves offer, then eventually, Compburo's orders would decline because their current clients will begin to hire their own staff. Also, with more skilled people entering the field, it is inevitable that new, cheaper computer-based design consultancies will enter the market. In fast-moving fields such as computer services and other industries connected with information technology, keeping up with current developments is much harder but also of more vital importance. In swiftly changing markets, growth can give way to decline with even greater speed.

Obviously, the main defences against being caught out – especially if you have committed yourself to heavy expenditure in anticipation of continued growth – are to monitor the market constantly (discussed in the next section) and to pick customers who value your products – whether goods or services – for a particular convenience or service that they feel your products provide. Even if market tastes suddenly switch, or a very attractive competitor enters your markets, well-satisfied customers (whether consumer, industrial or commercial) are not anxious to go through the inevitable disruptions involved in testing or seeking alternatives. However, customers who have been only partially satisfied with your service, or who feel that they were compelled to buy from you will certainly be willing to try competing products if they become available.

These effects of customer satisfaction–dissatisfaction are the major reasons why it is so important not only to maintain high-quality customer relations (which are often very hard to maintain during a period of rapid growth), but also to identify your 'natural' customers and those who provide your highest profits. A very well-known formula often cited in this context is the *80:20 rule*, which was mentioned in chapter 6. Very simply, in this context, the rule states that 80 per cent of sales or profits come from around 20 per cent of your customers. Of course, the 20 per cent who account for the bulk of your sales need not be the same 20 per cent who account for most of your profits, and it is quite clearly the latter who are the most important customers for your business. However, sometimes, particularly if your financial and sales records are not well kept or up to date, it is hard to identify your most profitable customers quickly and, if you want to act swiftly, it may be more practical to monitor your sales figures.

Whichever figures you decide to monitor, remember that your ultimate aim should always be to identify the core of your most profitable customer types. Also note that, although you will base your customer analysis on your actual customers (provided, of course, that they are easily identifiable, which they may not be if you have a retail business or sell via intermediaries), your intention should be to identify customer segments so that you can then target other customers in the most profitable segments.

However, in identifying your present profitable customer segments, you need also to anticipate what might happen to the most important segments, and decide if they are likely to continue to provide you with such profitable business in the future. Obvious questions to consider include: which products are likely to be in demand this year and in what way are the patterns of demand likely to change next year? You will also need to make some sort of forecast of likely future demand from each customer (which will be a function of each customer's own capacities and business prospects). To help the accuracy of your forecasts, it is also, of course, crucial to be in a position to identify any special seasonal or regional demands for any of your products. Another factor to bear in mind when identifying future customer segments is the economic and financial aspects of differences in spending behaviour of different groups.

Going back to the section on different levels of motivation, it is clear that the satisfaction of different types of needs or demands can have natural ceilings – perhaps associated with income, or with season, or in response to global, national or European trends. For instance, as people become relatively wealthier (not necessarily rich), they tend to spend proportionally less on *basic* food, clothing and shelter, and more on leisure, health products and, in some cases, *luxury* food, clothing and shelter. Generally, across parts of Western Europe and North America price considerations were of prime importance to mass markets during the first decades after the Second World War, but were followed by concerns over quality during succeeding decades and, more recently, design and uniqueness have become strong customer preferences, as previous mass markets have begun to segment. Because customers who are moving into higher-wage brackets or into a more affluent style of living seem to be more prepared to pay a premium for more specialized products, you need to know which of your products could be marketed to these types of customer. And, in addition, you should find out what factors determine the selling price and how price-sensitive your target future customers are likely to be. How to find much of this information is the subject of the following section.

Researching markets and trends

From the issues discussed in the previous section – and, indeed, in all the previous chapters – it should be becoming clear that you need to be very well informed if you are to manage your current growth problems satisfactorily and plan for future growth. No doubt you pick up useful items of business-relevant information just about every day of the week but, when you are trying to make decisions about important business problems, you really need to spend some time and effort in identifying your real alternatives, and in choosing the best option. For these purposes, therefore, research is no more than finding out as much relevant information about precise problems as you can.

However, unless you are in an industry where research is fairly commonplace, you may be one of many small-business owners who find that the term 'research' suggests impracticality and excessive consumption of time for little output. Certainly, a great deal of academic and government-related research studies does take a lot of time and often produces thick reports that are either very theoretical or over-burdened with detail. Fortunately, that type of research is at the other end of the spectrum, well away from the type of research that you need to solve your growth problems. At the business end of the spectrum (even if you run a research consultancy), research tends to be much more down to earth and virtually always serves a purely practical purpose – providing you with enough information to avoid making costly mistakes. This type of research can be extremely cheap and informal (keeping brochures sent from clients, competitors and suppliers and relevant cuttings of articles from magazines and newspapers), or rather expensive and professional (hiring a market research firm to test a potential new market), but it should always be focused on helping to solve practical and precisely defined business problems.

In fact, most of the information that you require to manage the growth of your business concerns customers, markets and products. Customers, who are not always the ultimate consumers, are constantly giving signals about what products they want to buy. Consumers also give fairly clear signals about the sort of products that will sell. However, you need to know where to find this information, how to gather it, and how to interpret it when you do find it. On the first question of where to gather such information, it is worth pointing out that there are a number of easily accessible internal and external sources that most businesses find give sufficient information for their immediate purposes. Indeed, the first place to start is right in your own business with your own records and, if you have any, your own sales staff.

Because they are constantly in contact with your customers and often have links with other organizations in your field of business, your sales staff should be providing you with a steady stream of feedback. Indeed, unless you have organized your central administrative functions along the lines suggested in chapter 4, you may find yourself swamped with information if you start encouraging them to report back on market shifts, intelligence on competitors and possible new customers. First, make sure that you have a system for processing and, very importantly, acting on the information that you receive, then begin to encourage your sales staff to start gathering useful information (a bonus for new customers or warnings about new competing products would help). The sort of questions they could be asking need not be too complicated, but more along the lines of: 'why do you buy our product?' 'what can we do to improve it?' 'why did you not buy our latest product?' 'have you had any approaches from other suppliers?' and so on. Your own suppliers are also a good source for finding out about general technical and business developments in your field – not only because they see a wider range of your industry than you might but also because they generally like getting feedback themselves. Finally, in this rather informal research network, do not ignore your non-sales staff. They should be part of your intelligence system, picking up information from friends who work in similar businesses and other sources. Delivery staff and office staff often hear a great deal during their working day.

There is usually no problem about getting people to give this level of information – indeed customers are normally happy to tell you directly what products and services they like or dislike. However, it must be stressed that your organization should be geared so that it can collect and use this information. For instance, sales staff should be responsible for reporting on sales gained, customers lost and sales not made. This information should be collected by your office – or, eventually, by your sales office, if your business reaches the appropriate size – then channelled to you or whoever is responsible for controlling the marketing efforts, so that action can be taken. At the same time, you or your office staff should be regularly monitoring sales records, delivery and stock records, prices and quotations, plus noting who is quick and who is slow to respond to orders and invoices. Also, your administrative staff should be keeping copies or cuttings of local and national sales promotions, advertising, analysis of costs and results, salesmen's reports, newspaper and magazine articles and even previously published market research studies.

Although much of this internal research system relies on fairly informal methods, there is also plenty of quite sophisticated sleuthing that you can undertake, provided your records are accurate, accessible and up to date. For instance, the 80:20 analysis mentioned in the previous section and in chapter 6 can provide you with the most effective information for managing your business – for stock control, debtor control, identifying customer segments, monitoring the development of products and a number of other tasks that are unique to your business. At some point, however, especially if you are about to spend large sums of money on developing new products or entering new markets, you need to gather information from external sources so that you can take the most sensible decisions. When you start to move outside your business for information, the research process becomes more formal and has to be even more precisely targeted.

Of course, if you have to give a research brief to an outside agency, you have to treat them as you would any other professional – give clear instructions, make sure everything that you want covered is included in the fee, and make sure that the agency delivers everything that you expect in a form that you can understand. This reinforces the point made in chapter 5 that you pay fees to professional advisers on the expectation of receiving specific advice or services and, in accepting your money, they undertake to provide you with the information you seek to your satisfaction, provided you were sufficiently clear in your original instructions. With most professional advisers – accountants, solicitors, surveyors, architects, designers and so on – it is much easier to agree a reasonably precise brief, but research outcomes are not so easy to predict and, more often than not, pose more questions than they answer. Therefore, it is particularly important – especially if you are only now beginning to emerge from a period of unplanned, reactive growth but are unsure about your future direction – to make sure that you understand all you can find out about your current and intended markets before approaching a research agency. You do not want to pay a hefty fee and later find that all they did was provide you with information that you could have found by yourself in any well-stocked business library.

Indeed, before approaching an agency, conduct a search of available published data such as reports by consumer organizations, government statistics, census data, national income figures, family expenditure surveys, trade association data, published surveys and sector reports conducted by national organizations such as the National Economic Development Office and by business journals such as *The Economist, British Business, The Financial Times* and so on. There is a lot of information published regularly – perhaps too much – and most business libraries have access to it. Local libraries are now connected to each other by on-line data links and you can usually order locally reports held by bigger business libraries. Even if you cannot get the entire report, you can often pay for extracts or photocopies of relevant pages (so long as this does not infringe the Copyright Act). Most of this type of external information can be gathered directly by your own staff and can be very valuable.

Once you are satisfied that you have learned all that is practical to find from your own internal and publicly available sources, the next stage is to consider using external agencies or commercial data sources. If you are interested in finding new distributors or suppliers (or even potential partners in a joint venture), most of the well-known trade directories (*Kompass, Kelly's*, and so on) plus a number of newer – often internationally based – directories (for instance, *Dun and Bradstreet*) now operate on-line services so that you can find suitable firms in specific regions and industries. Indeed, these directories usually also provide the names, business addresses and telephone numbers of managing directors, sales directors, purchasing managers and other key members of staff so that you can also identify potential customers and clients. Again, your staff can liaise with these data sources and process much of the information for you. For the next step of actually commissioning a research study, however, you would be well advised to make sure that you are personally involved.

It is very important to be sure of exactly what you are looking for and how you will use the information before calling in a market research expert. Market research agencies are useful for identifying different types of consumers or customers (especially for retailing or consumer goods businesses) and, if they use suitable techniques, for finding out why customers purchase (or do not purchase) your products and what are the key attributes of your products that appeal to your target markets. Research agencies can also be useful for identifying competitors and calculating your share of the total market. All these issues require careful thought and you need to be clear about what you want to find out and why. You also do not want to be paying for answers that you are unlikely to use.

There is not much point in agreeing an elaborate and expensive research project – including surveys, consumer panels, experiments, test marketing of products and competitor analyses – if the expected outcome will only yield information that is of marginal interest to you or of little help in deciding future strategy for your business. By the same token, if the information is vital for arriving at a very important and even more expensive decision, then you must be prepared to pay a reasonable price to obtain the best-quality information. To repeat, however, always insist on getting value for money – especially if you are relying on the information to tell you about new markets (next section) or to help in developing new products (pp. 117–122).

Managing declining products

As a general strategy for most smaller independent businesses, it seems clear that a series of incremental modifications to existing main products, processes or markets is the best course of action for managing continued growth. Certainly you can maintain your position in the market by actively modifying your products and services in response to the inevitable shifts in market taste. However, your main reason for buying this book may have been that your main product has recently begun to experience a drop in sales or profits or both. Most of the previous chapters should have been useful in pointing out strategies and management considerations of future growth, but your immediate concern will be with how to halt the decline of your main product and, hence, that of your business. Indeed, even if your main product is not yet actually declining, when you start pushing resources into new (see next section) or modified products it is likely that sales in the original product will begin to taper off. Either way, it is imperative that you have strategies for managing declining products as part of your overall growth strategy. The future implications of these issues are discussed in the next chapter and, in this section, it is mainly the question of what to do with a declining product that is examined.

Once you believe that any one of your products (or derivative product lines) is reaching a period of relative stability in sales and development, it is likely that the product is entering the *maturity* phase of the life cycle and you should begin to plan its replacement. Eventually, on the downward, *decline* part of the product's life cycle, sales start to dip as either demand slows or competitors become more successful. For many industrial products, their life cycles can be measured in years but, for fashion items and similar fads, the life cycle can be quite short, with only days separating growth from decline. Up till now, however, we have only really used the concept of the product life cycle for descriptive purposes to explain where your products or business might be currently positioned.

However, life-cycle curves can be useful for budgeting and forecasting purposes. By plotting the previous sales of your products over past periods (months, quarters or years, depending on the type of goods or services), curves can instantly reveal seasonal variations. Also, if you have sufficient data to plot your sales patterns from when your product was launched, a dipping curve can suggest what sales pattern you might expect for future periods unless some corrective action is taken. Of course, to use your own sales curves to full advantage, you should also take the trouble to find out what has been happening to sales of all similar products in the wider market, so that you can compare your own product's performance, and take a view on likely future prospects for sales overall.

If your curve has stabilized for several periods but recently started to dip, you need to find out why in a hurry, especially if your sales are declining in an external stable or buoyant market. Your first step should be to look internally to your pricing structures, to the efficiency of your office or sales staff in responding to orders or clients and to your methods of distribution and promotion. These issues have been discussed in previous chapters and most are covered in greater depth in *The Barclays Guide to Marketing for the Small Business*. But, even if the overall market is contracting, if you find your curve is dipping more steeply than the market as a whole, you need to take steps to ensure that your decline is less severe than that of your competition, so that you have more time and resources to develop more suitable products or find other markets.

Therefore, apart from tightening up your internal procedures, you will need to know why the market is contracting (competition, temporary or longer-term economic downturn, outdated technology, shift in consumer tastes, and so on), and what the medium- and longer-term prospects are. It may be that your decline curve is markedly less steep than the total market decline, but that you feel the writing is on the wall for the total sector. This could happen to our fictitious examples Compburo, if more skilled and trained people start entering the corporate labour market, and Batchjob, if their main jobbing contractors start to produce themselves or source their main components in lower-cost countries such as Portugal or Spain. In both cases, the owners have already begun to develop their businesses towards higher-value products with brighter future prospects. There are plenty of other strategic issues to take into account when planning such shifts in direction, but life-cycle curves can give important clues to enable you to manipulate the life cycles of your products to your advantage.

However, if you do decide that, despite your best efforts, the future for your product is bleak – you are selling your goods or services reasonably efficiently but the main markets for your products are in fundamentally bad shape – you cannot just drop your product unless you want to close your business. And, even with this worst case scenario, your troubles may not end there, if you have outstanding creditors and staff to be paid off. (Both *The Barclays Guide to Law for the Small Business* and *The Barclays Guide to Managing Staff for the Small Business* cover the technical aspects of closing your business.) If you are still ambitious for your business to grow (once again, back to your personal business ambitions), you need to buy time and conserve resources by managing your declining product carefully. You may even find that the sales dip was temporary and that your main product has several years of life left.

The most sensible strategy is to try and increase your *market penetration* by either increasing market share or finding new markets. This basically involves keeping your existing customers and finding new ones in the same market or similar ones in new markets. In turn, this means that your pricing and promotion will have to be very competitive, because other suppliers are not just going to sit back and let you take their business. However, if you feel that you understand your markets well, you could consider the modification of your current products to improve their quality, style, or whatever characteristics are valued by customers.

This, in turn, returns us to your need to understand your markets and what makes your current customers buy your goods or services. The aim of this strategy is to extend or develop your existing markets by finding new customers or consumers for your goods or users of your services. This might mean going further afield geographically either abroad (exporting) or to neighbouring regions or, if you are currently mainly local, deciding to launch your product on a national basis. For any of these options, especially the third one, you will need to conduct sufficient research of your intended markets to justify the inevitable expenditure – not only of finance but also of staffing resource including yourself.

Basically, a strategy aimed at increasing market share means that you are still relying on your old product – even though you may have extended its life by a few years. If you feel that its longer-term future in its current form is still in doubt, a slightly more innovative approach might be to explore the possibilities of opening up new market segments or finding new applications for your products. Indeed, at some point, the strategy of increasing your market share for your existing products will lead you to understand that your market is actually composed of several segments. This means that you may be able to identify other, similar segments that you have not yet tried. Again, this will prolong the life of your product without significantly altering it. However, unless you find some genuinely new uses for your product, eventually you are likely to realize that, to stand any real chance of making significant improvements to your sales, you will need to modify your product for each segment.

It is important to bear in mind, however, that each action that extends the period of growth for your basic product costs money and has to be weighed against the level of increased sales. Indeed, even as you contemplate how to find new markets or how to exploit more fully your existing market segments, you should also be thinking of the organizational and financial implications. Sooner or later, you will be faced with two decisions – financial and organizational – because the resources required to keep the older product alive will begin to compete with the resources needed to develop newer products. Of course, you will not enter a new market or consider a new segment if the expected increase in sales would not produce a profit but, even so, the costs of locating a new market or servicing a new segment will eventually block the development or marketing of a new product. Before that point arrives, you have to decide a budget for maintaining your original product and a separate budget for developing any proposed new product (indeed, it would be better to have a separate budget for each new market or segment penetration).

Organizationally, you will then be in a position to decide whether you will take personal charge of maintaining the older product or developing new products. Whichever you decide to do, having separate budgets will allow you – indeed it should be your own management priority – to delegate the other main task to someone else. But, this delegation must be a genuine one of authority as well as tasks (including, however, regular feedback and the monitoring of performance against the budgets).

Eventually, there comes a time when you begin to run out of new markets or separate segments in your existing markets, and it becomes counter-productive to prop up your ailing products or services. Before you arrive at this point, however, the most obvious strategy for a growing business such as yours is to start developing new, profitable products, to take up the slack as your older products decline. Once one of your products has ceased growing and significantly slipped in market share (known as a *dog* in the marketing world), you must avoid wasting more money on it, even if some apparently lucrative opportunities present themselves, because almost inevitably it will be more profitable for you to develop a specific new product to meet that opportunity. Indeed, if there is a captive market for the old product, you should actually raise its price to generate more development funds for other products and to kill it off more quickly. The main issues involved in this wider growth strategy are covered in the next chapter, while the techniques of new product development are discussed in the following section.

Developing new products

The importance of not entrusting the fate of your business to one product has been emphasized at several points throughout this book (especially in chapter 2, p. 25, and earlier in this chapter on p. 105). However, if your business depends on your own expertise in a particular field or on a product in a well-defined market, it may seem difficult to develop a completely new or different product.

Indeed, it would be a mistake to sell another product or offer another service merely because it was a novelty. Developing a new product, however, need not be quite so dramatic. One consistent piece of advice offered by this book on how to handle the unforeseen problems of growth has been to encourage you to switch from a product-oriented approach to a more customer-oriented approach. Your search for a compatible new product with a reasonable potential for success is just an extension of this change in orientation.

There are a number of techniques which are useful for developing new products without going through the uncertain agonies of inventing a totally new one. In practice most new products and services emerge gradually from modifications of existing ideas and technology, from putting together familiar things in a slightly different way. It is this interplay between existing products or services and the search for improvement and innovation which can sustain the dynamism in a growing business like yours. Basically, you face a choice of remaining with existing markets and customers, or else finding new ones, and your main strategy options are either to modify your existing products and markets, or to find new ones. The combination of these options gives rise to a number of broad strategies.

Once you arrive at the point where you realize that your current market can be split into different segments, you are faced with a choice of options. First, you can modify your basic product to produce specific lines or models for each segment. Secondly, you can look more closely at what benefits your most profitable segments are seeking when they buy or use your products, with the aim of introducing a new product which meets their needs even more. Finally, you can decide to identify your target segments – ideally those that offer the greatest volumes of sales at high profits – and concentrate on providing them with a whole range of suitable products. Essentially, these three options are further developments of the same theme, and the level that you decide is appropriate for your business will depend on your available resources and marketing strengths.

If you are contemplating a new market or modifications to your existing products, you need to conduct a *product-gap analysis* to ensure that you are putting your energies and resources into the most productive areas. To conduct such an analysis, list your main products and services in a column, and your principal markets along the top of a sheet of paper. The rows and columns for each product and market will intersect to form little squares or boxes. In each appropriate small square, write in your current annual sales revenue and your target annual sales revenue for the coming year. Take a note of your current total target sales forecast, then add up the target sales for each column and row. You should be able to see which products and which markets are your strong points and which ones look weak (and either need attention or to be dropped – see the previous section).

Any obvious gaps reveal your potential need for a good product for that market. Of course, you need to ask yourself some fundamental questions to identify the precise nature of the product gap (and, as mentioned above in a previous section, this is an area where market research can help). First, you need to know whether there is a real customer need for any new product or service and what sort of demand it is likely to be. You will also need to know whether you should be aiming at new or existing customers and how to reach any new customers. If you feel there is a strong case for a new product or service, you have to decide how it fits in with your existing range and whether you have the resources or expertise to provide it (and, of course, how much it will cost to implement). Finally, you will need to address the negative side, such as what the competition provides and what the result will be if you fail to provide it. If you consider these questions and still decide to go ahead, but do not have a suitable product or service that you could modify, then you will have to start considering how to innovate and diversify.

Diversification is the most risky strategy of all, since you are forced to deal with new markets as well as learn about your new products and services. Dealing with so many unknown elements increases your risk – roughly 90 per cent of new products are said to fail – and, if you are drawn to such a strategy, make sure that you subject your plans to very careful evaluation. Above all, even if you have developed a brilliant new idea for a product or service and you are convinced that it is appropriate for you to move rapidly to exploit your new idea, be careful that you do not take on too much. A small company with its limited resources may well find itself stretched if it tries too many new things at once. By spreading yourself too thinly, you cannot hope to make a strong impact in any one area.

The least risky way of dealing with the development of new products and services is not to innovate, or to seek completely new ideas, but to pick up on successful ideas that have been implemented elsewhere. By adopting this strategy, you can avoid all the costs associated with developing the new ideas and creating the markets for them. Instead, you can take an idea from some other region or country and modify it to meet the needs of a more local market and to fit in with your capacity. There should be no stigma associated with this type of copying because it is how products and culture spread from one economy to another. Indeed, a number of businesses – provided they can negotiate satisfactory royalties or fees – are actually pleased for other businesses to manufacture or market their products. Indeed, many manufacturers enter into joint ventures on this basis and, more commonly these days, many services find that franchising out their business is actually an efficient way to manage their own rapid growth (see *The Barclays Guide to Franchising for the Small Business*). Consequently, keep your eyes and ears open when speaking to suppliers, customers or competitors, and always look around when you are taking a foreign trip. You should also monitor technical or trade journals for technological innovations. If the product is based on a national product or on another existing product already in your market, you can take advantage of the interest in the product created by the innovator. The key to success with this strategy is timing. Too early and you may get stuck with relatively high start-up costs and no proof that the product is a success; too late and the market for the idea may have gone. However, the inherent flexibility of your business should enable it to adjust to the most suitable timing, making this strategy quite attractive.

Indeed, faced with a changing environment, the flexibility of most small businesses is tested to the full. Just as you can analyse the services or goods you sell in terms of the product life cycle (see chapter 2, pp. 24–5 and the first section of this chapter), so you can look at your business in the same way. During the early stages, with personal decision-making in small groups, it is possible to respond swiftly to changing events. As the business grows and matures, there is a danger that the decision-making remains too personal and resistant to change. You may find that innovation or even product modification is difficult to implement, not so much because of technical difficulties, but because members of your staff are not ready or else feel threatened by change. It is this failure to adapt to growth that blocks the expansion of many small businesses. Flexibility requires a system in which new ideas flourish and are capable of being quickly tested and smoothly implemented. Such a system, which is described in chapter 4, is encouraged by a participative leadership style, but inhibited by over-structuring. Indeed, the real benefits of participation to many small businesses are more likely to lie in this promotion of flexibility and innovation than in any potential increases in productivity.

People will only advance new ideas and constructively discuss those of other people if they know that they will get a genuine and supportive hearing themselves. However, you also need a reasonable flow of feasible ideas for new products or services. The potential sources of new ideas for products and services are virtually boundless, ranging from a sudden insight through to some very analytical techniques. The key sources of new product ideas are likely to be based on research and development and market search. Attractive though they might seem, successful ideas generated by creative thinking techniques have been fairly limited, because they are likely to be product-oriented rather than customer-oriented. For instance, brainstorming – a technique which involves a group of people thinking through new uses to which a product or service can be put – can generate a lot of useful ideas, but there is little attempt to decide which of them are at all practical. The key to brainstorming is that all ideas are listed and judgement about their feasibility is suspended until a large number of ideas have been generated.

There are a number of other creative techniques, such as lateral thinking, which examines familiar ideas and tries to turn them back to front. For example, Compburo may have started to offer designed products or design facilities to corporate clients but, in recognizing their own staffing problems, identify a profitable niche as a specialist temporary employment agency. In other words, instead of providing bigger corporations with design expertise and so saving them staffing costs, Compburo ends up providing staff for big corporations to complete their in-house designing. Also, it is very profitable if you can think of new applications of new materials or new technology. The obvious examples are the use of new plastic materials or high-strength resins as substitutes for more expensive, metal products.

If you are keen to develop new products, you need to think of as many different methods as you can which could be the source of ideas for new products or services. Then write your thoughts on a sheet of paper and discuss them with friends and colleagues. Your original ideas may not have been so good but the criticisms may spark off a genuinely interesting new product idea. Indeed, it may pay you to set up a regular ideas session with family, staff, friends and appropriate outsiders. You need to keep in touch with what your competitors are doing. You need to monitor – as we discuss in the following chapter – new legislation, especially that which relates to safety, the environment or crime reduction. You need to monitor which imported products are selling well and driving out local competition. All these areas can be potent sources of new products or services.

One point to note is that successful innovators have a much better understanding of user needs than their less successful contemporaries. One of their techniques is to list the attributes of a product or service, and then modify them in the search for an improved version. This can be similar to the market or product-gap analysis mentioned above. Also, analysing past sales figures for significant trends can lead you to new ideas for future products. After that, you could also consider conducting specific market research, perhaps leading to new ways of segmentation, which could also generate new product or service ideas. There are certainly plenty of sources for new ideas although you should take care that they are viable. As you begin to plan and bring on stream new products or start introducing new services, however, you must also decide what to do about your original products, especially if they are even now giving signs that they are running out of steam. Developing a coherent strategy for the future growth of your business embraces the need to manage innovation while simultaneously forestalling the onset of decay, and this is covered in the last two chapters.

Summary

This chapter has gone beyond the problems posed by immediate growth and has looked more closely into the strategies and techniques for dealing with present and future growth. In a sense, this chapter has laid the groundwork on which you can plan and manage the future growth of your business. As a result of the material covered in this chapter you should now be able to analyse what the development of your products means in terms of your own management priorities.

Key points

- Identify your key growth customers according to their effects on your sales and profits.
- Identify your key customer segments according to the characteristics of your key growth customers.
- Use internal and external sources of information to identify similar market segments.
- Use research agencies when you need to know finer details about your customers or markets, but make sure that you give them a clear brief.
- Make sure that you have exploited all the profitable markets and segments for your older products before dropping them in favour of newer products.
- Aim to have new products growing as your old products decline.

8

Developing your future growth strategy

Outline

Having analysed your own growth problems and addressed the key issues that you need to take into account in overcoming them, you are now on a firm base for looking ahead. The previous three chapters have prepared the ground, and the main aim of this chapter is to help you construct a model of how you see your future business expansion. We consider:

- the value of having a balanced portfolio of products and services
- the need to remain on guard against competition, sudden market switches and changes to your business environment
- different approaches towards dealing with changes in your capital and labour needs
- the need to take into account external influences such as changes in new technology and the Single Market
- the need to develop a system for retaining the personal values of your business as you organize it for growth

In a sense, this chapter represents a new beginning, or the point from which you could have started if your business growth had been planned. The whole purpose of business planning is to remove some of the uncertainty facing your business, by systematically assessing and preparing for the future. To guarantee adequate flexibility, you need to monitor all the key areas of your business (the organizational, financial and marketing issues discussed in previous chapters) and, if you spot any warning signals, you need to be prepared to introduce changes even when things appear to be going smoothly.

Obviously, in such circumstances, you also need to be sure in your own mind that the quality of the information upon which you base your decisions is reliable. In turn, this means that you also have to keep checking that your longer-term goals and shorter-term objectives remain valid, because, ultimately, your decisions are aimed at attaining those targets. Therefore, the sections in this chapter look at various internal and external influences on your business and how to anticipate future trends and retain personal commitment as your business grows.

Keeping ahead of your competition

It is not enough to be growing at the moment or controlling your recent growth. You need to be able to ensure that you can continue to grow at the pace that you set for your business. The skills, techniques and strategies required to control the pace and direction of your business growth have been covered extensively throughout this book. However, your business does not exist in isolation and, as the previous chapter should have made clear, you need to take into account the outside world whenever you are planning a major new business activity. As part of becoming customer-oriented you also have to be aware of your competitors.

The practical side of identifying your competitors and estimating their share of your total markets (and their main customers and suppliers) is a research problem which was covered in the last chapter (pp. 108–13). The subject of this section is how to ensure that you have a sufficiently balanced portfolio of products and customer segments to withstand competition from any quarter, and a strong base from which to grow. As you grow, one of your aims should be to avoid becoming over-dependent on any one area of your business, so that it is hard for a sudden market shift to knock you off-balance.

The need to start developing new products while managing the decline of your older products has already been discussed in the previous chapter, but the notion of a balanced portfolio goes beyond merely replacing aging products with new ones. The aim is to have a number of compatible and profitable products at different stages of development, with enough resources in reserve to respond to new opportunities in related fields. Of course, your portfolio of products, which basically rests on your ability to provide different products that satisfy the needs of a variety of market segments, could easily include a mix of goods and services. For instance, Batchjob might consider installation, maintenance and even marketing services in connection with their own and other manufacturers' industrial goods, while Compburo may be in the position to take up a number of profitable distribution agencies for CAD and CAM machines as well as other ancillary products. It is already common for some manufacturers to have linked wholesale or retail outlets and for certain services to sell the products that are used in providing their service.

How to achieve a reasonably balanced mix of products is covered in *The Barclays Guide to Marketing for the Small Business*, where useful methods for classifying products according to, say, their growth prospects and their market share are more fully explained. The basic aim for a business that is beginning to outgrow its early dependence on its original product is to develop a range of different products appealing to various market segments, with one type of product generating development funds for its successor. Of course, the total portfolio of products must be profitable, and early action must be taken against products that threaten to affect the stability of your business or use up more than their fair share of resources. Apart from the low growth, low market share dogs (mentioned on p. 117), you will also want to avoid too many low market share, high growth *problem children*, which eat up development and promotional costs but do not generate much revenue. Some of these may turn into your target high market share, high growth *stars*, but many will not and they could ultimately become a net drain on your cash flow.

If you have recently been experiencing fairly rapid growth with a product that has high market share but fairly low further growth prospects – this type of product has been termed a *cash cow* – you can profit from the fact that you still enjoy relatively high sales with virtually no development or promotion costs. Because the cash cow is a net contributor to company revenue, provided you maintain your market position, you can manage the product to maximize your earnings. As hinted in the previous chapter, the key to classifying your products correctly, according to their growth and revenue prospects, lies in your ability to identify more markets or different segments for each product. Consequently, it is usually easier to distinguish your products (and this holds true for both goods and services) on the basis of their stage of development and market segments. Your chances of successfully seeing off your current and future competitors, including those that come with the new Single Market, depend strongly on your ability to spot openings for your products and to cover any important gaps.

This ability, in turn, is helped by a reasonable awareness of your customers' purchasing motivations. To reinforce the point made several times during this book, if you are to continue selling your products and services you need to know your customers well. Most of the effective techniques for monitoring the market and identifying important customers have been covered on pp. 108–113 of the previous chapter. As you begin to develop a strategy for your future growth, however, you need to decide exactly what sort of customers you want to serve, what products you want to specialize in, and how you want your business to be perceived by the outside world (this aspect of your future business strategy is discussed below on pp. 143–8, a section which describes the benefits and techniques of developing a corporate culture). For the moment, it is useful to consider what motivates and satisfies your most important customers.

As mentioned in chapter 4 (pp. 64–70), motivation basically depends on the strength of belief that a certain outcome or activity will satisfy an important need. This holds true for your staff – in relation to work motivation – and for your customers if you can convince them that your products will help them satisfy some of their important needs. Indeed, it is this potential to satisfy that you need to identify and sell as the key *benefit* of your product (see chapter 7, pp. 117–22 on developing new products). Needs, satisfaction and motivation, however, are quite complex and can be analysed on a number of different levels, starting from fundamental physical needs (food, drink, security, shelter, etc.), through a wide range of needs developed in response to our dealings with other people (including family and friends) and, often, to more psychological, internal needs connected with feelings of self-value and establishing a purpose in life.

Many management writers have classified levels of need into a progression of five linked categories – in ascending order:

- *physiological* needs such as hunger or thirst
- *safety* needs such as for security or stability
- *social* needs for supportive contact with other people

- *status* needs associated with respect, prestige or achievement
- *self-actualization* needs for a more human accomplishment, leading to feelings of self-worth and self-fulfilment

But there is no evidence that so-called lower-level needs have to be satisfied before the higher-level needs come into play. Also, these five categories actually overlap to a large extent, and there is plenty of evidence that people operate on various levels at the same time. Nevertheless, this five-way classification does provide a useful tool for analysing customer (and staff) behaviour.

Customers will first try to satisfy basic needs such as hunger or security before wanting to satisfy the higher-level needs such as status, respect or self-fulfilment. It is not just for economic reasons, therefore, that it is no use trying to sell financial services or hand-crafted shoes to someone who has not got the price of a meal. Even if they suddenly do come into some money, people who have been deprived of their basic needs – for instance many longer-term unemployed who have recently found work – will want to make sure that basics such as reasonable food, housing, heating and clothing are taken care of before contemplating buying less economically necessary items such as a car or washing-machine. They may, however, make several 'non-economic' or impulse purchases if they feel a need to boost their morale after their period of deprivation. Generally speaking, however, as economies develop and societies change, more people find that their basic needs are satisfied, and increasing numbers of consumers seek satisfaction for their higher needs (which is one reason why quality-of-life and environmental issues are now coming to the fore). Indeed, economists have long recognized that increased affluence leads to quite pronounced switches in consumption patterns (away from food to consumer goods, for instance), and that the consumption of some goods and services (mainly those that can be perceived as luxury or status goods) actually goes against commonsense and increases when the price is raised. With the rise in importance of 'green' and environmental issues, it may be expected that these previously noted patterns of consumption will begin to change and that new patterns of consumer behaviour will come to the fore. It is essential, therefore, if you are serious about planning your future growth, that you make strenuous efforts to understand why your customers buy your products.

Question 15 Which of the five levels of customers' needs do you feel that your current products mainly satisfy?

You may be able to answer this question straight away because you have targeted your goods or services at particular customers. If you are not sure, you should read *The Barclays Guide to Marketing for the Small Business*, especially the chapters on features and benefits and customer segmentation. For your planning purposes, however, you should make sure that you know where and how well your consumers' more basic needs were being met before they became your customers and where your ex-customers have tended to move on to. Markets are always changing and, as we have discussed, economic developments alter customers' attitudes and motivational profiles across quite wide areas. You only need to look at any fad or change in fashion to see how quickly customer behaviour can change.

For instance, look at how smoking has fallen out of favour in Britain and how health foods and environmental-related products have taken off. Remember, the fact that you have experienced unexpected growth is no guarantee that your business growth will continue. You have to monitor customer tastes and preferences constantly. Also, as attitudes change, you need to work out how the changes are likely to affect your goods or services, whether there are any business lessons to be learnt from the past, and if the changes that have occurred have taken place mainly because of external economic changes (such as the Single Market, which will be discussed in a later section). In general, you need to know what factors affect your social and business environment, if you are to understand the pattern of customer behaviour. Customers form their opinions from a wide range of sources, and how they perceive the changing world will alter their attitudes towards most issues. More importantly, from the viewpoint of your business, how customer attitudes change vitally affects how they respond to your goods and services rather than those of your competitors.

By developing a strong customer-orientation, you will address such issues as customer service, convenience, reliable delivery and a host of similar issues as a matter of course. If you have been coping with the problems of growth until recently, you may not have had the time or energy to attend to such important issues. Hopefully, as you complete this book, you will now be able to pay attention to such matters as your customers' expectations of help and free advice, or whether your premises are warm and well laid out with your range of goods or services clearly displayed. Although it is relatively easy to see how these notions of customer service apply to service businesses and retailers, the same attitudes are appropriate for manufacturers, where the easy maintenance and repair of your products, not to mention the quality of your after-sales service, could become important factors in your ultimate business success. These issues are picked up again in this chapter (pp. 143–8, on the need to develop a corporate culture). In the next sections, some of the internal and external factors that influence the pattern of your future growth are considered, starting with the need to clear away redundant features of your past business so that you can concentrate on the present and the future.

Clearing the decks

To attain maximum efficiency, you need to be concentrating on the markets you feel that your business should enter, and on the products which produce your profits. This means that the resources of your business should not be wasted on irrelevant activities and that all your marketing efforts should be focused on achieving your current goals. Since your position on the business life cycle is an indication of your current staffing and financial resources as well as your own managerial professionalism, your current styles and techniques of marketing, production and organization will also tend to reflect both your current position on it and your anticipated future position. Consequently, your resources needs are going to be changing constantly as you move up the growth curve. Some of your existing resources, particularly your key staff and other people and equipment associated with your core functions, will adapt to the new and changing needs of your business. However, some resources will not be capable of use in the new areas.

This means that, as your business grows, if you are to maintain your business efficiency, you will need to prune not only weak products (the dogs and most problem children) but also other redundant features of your business. These can include unsuitable premises and machines and equipment associated with discontinued products, as well as staff who resist training and do not fit in. What you may consider as redundant will naturally depend on your growth products and your personal business goals, but, once you have planned the future course that you expect your business to take, you have to decide how to achieve your goals and objectives as efficiently as possible. Essentially, this breaks down into two main tasks. The principal task involves you and your key staff in setting priorities, time-tables and costing your preferred strategies, while you also conduct the more constant monitoring task of ensuring that your future business conforms to the areas that fit your growth plan.

One of the main effects of allowing growth to occur without planning is that often unprofitable and wasteful activities and products develop alongside the growth areas (or, still worse, in competition with them). Indeed, much of this book – especially these final two chapters – is about identifying these non-growth aspects of your business. Tidying up these loose organizational ends is the first serious step on the path towards producing an effective growth plan. In fact, many of these important business issues need to be treated in some depth and are covered by the other Barclays Guides already mentioned throughout this book. The essential point made by this section is that, while capital (equipment, finance, premises, raw materials and other, similar items) and labour have to be treated differently, the requirements for both will alter as your business grows, and they both have to be managed appropriately if the past is not to block the future.

The essential difference between how you treat capital and labour is that labour really means people, and people have to be treated with respect and according to the law whereas capital items can be treated as objects – in that they can be quantified, analysed and simply removed or transformed according to financial criteria. Fixed assets, such as machines, vehicles or buildings, are expensive to buy and maintain, and a common method of measuring how well they are being used is to see how many pounds' worth of sales each pound of fixed assets is generating. Although the nature of the assets will vary from business to business, it is usually not too difficult to calculate (or have your accountant calculate) an overall ratio for all your assets, and individual ratios for each main category of assets (and thus identify the items or categories that under-perform). Although the techniques for calculating these ratios, and their interpretation, are covered in *The Barclays Guide to Financial Management for the Small Business*, their importance from a management view-point is not mathematical but informational. They can be another early warning signal that one of your products is entering its stage of decline. By comparing these ratios against the previous or budgeted usage, you will be able to see if there has been any decline or improvement. Before deciding to jettison any equipment, however, you will also need to know how frequently the equipment is normally used and how central it is to the way your production is organized – and which machines have excessive repair and main-tenance costs.

For instance, our fictional example Batchjob, which is organized to produce batches of products on different machines to satisfy various orders, will be more flexible and less tied to any single piece of equipment than an engineer organized on a job production or flow production basis. Manufacturers organized to produce single large jobs, where complete products are made at one place and one time, will need to ensure that vital machines are up to scratch. So too will bigger firms that need to keep their production constantly running. Companies organized for flow production, where produc-tion of parts is continuous for complete shifts, are also more vulnerable to shifts in the market, because their products are often made for stock rather than for particular customers. Taking all these factors into account, individual pieces of equipment can be compared and their usage, maintenance and replacement controlled to the maximum benefit of the business.

A primary objective of most businesses is to make a satisfactory level of return on capital employed (ROCE). As you grow, however, you will also want to know the likely future return on your current investment, so that you can plan and select the best options. In fact, this type of analysis comes into its own when deciding on new capital investment proposals, where money is expended today and revenues come into the business over a period of years. The various alternative forms of analysis to help with this longer-term planning are explained more fully in *The Barclays Guide to Financial Manage-ment for the Small Business*, but the main methods, in order of complexity, are:

- averaging the rate of return
- calculating the payback period

- the discounted cash-flow method (the method most preferred by accountants but least used by owners of new or smaller businesses)

The simplest method is to average your expected return on capital over a period of time, say the next five years. By calculating an *average return on capital employed* (ARCE), you can work out if any proposed investment during the next five years is likely to increase or reduce your average rate of return. However, this method does not distinguish clearly the different cash-flow profiles of the various elements of your product portfolio which offer similar average rates of return. Nor does it take into account the stronger preference for current cash than for the same amount of cash at, say, five years in the future. *Payback*, in essence a break-even on the purchase costs of the investment, provides a good estimate of the time taken for the original cost to be recovered. Thus, Batchjob may need a particular machine tool, costing £100,000, if it is to compete for specialized small-batch contracts. The projected annual net cash inflows may be £20,000, £40,000 and £40,000 (i.e., a total of £100,000), yielding a payback period of three years. However, the payback method may not identify which investment is likely to generate more positive cash inflows over the period if two investments have the same payback period nor does it take into account the effects of *time preference* for money.

The discounted cash-flow method meets both of these objections by looking at the whole life of the project and applying *present value factors* to convert future revenues into current values. As this method is the one that appeals to many sources of finance that you may approach, it will pay you to find out more about it than this brief outline provides. For our present purposes, however, we can use the Batchjob example to illustrate briefly how discounted cash-flow works. If Batchjob's owner calculates that flows from the new investment will taper off after three years but still bring in an extra £40,000 annually over the next two years, with operating costs taken into account, it looks like clear profit of £80,000. However, if inflation is high and future flows of money are less desirable than those of today, we need to compensate for this 'time preference'. Also, the expected returns on alternative investments have to be taken into account. Thus, Batchjob's owner may expect a return on investment of 20 per cent (say, double a deposit savings interest of 10 per cent) so the value of future cash inflows from current investment in new plant must be discounted to take into account the forgone current return on other potential investments. Batchjob's accountant can use present interest rates and inflation rates (or even the published discount rates that are available for this purpose) to calculate the net present value of the cash inflow and perhaps find that the investment – with its profit of £80,000 coming after four inflation-hit years – is not so profitable after all. Indeed, as a crude comparison, without taking into account inflation or time-preference factors, a bank deposit of £100,000 at 10 per cent over five years would have returned around £60,000 without risk and Batchjob's expected 20 per cent over five years would be roughly £150,000 on an investment of £100,000. To subject your own current capital equipment and future investment plans to this useful, rigorous examination consult your accountant.

Returning now to the question of how growth affects your labour requirements, however, it must be said that your accountant may not always offer the best advice (though the financial effects of your labour costs should always be taken into account). People are the most important asset in any business, and as such they must be monitored closely to get the best out of them. They must be trained – especially if they are new to your business – not only to do their current jobs, but also to prepare them for promotion or new responsibilities. Although the law relating to unfair dismissals and industrial relations has been relaxed to help small firms, especially those with fewer than 10 employees (see *The Barclays Guide to Law for the Small Business*), the courts require that certain minimal procedures be followed. Employees must know their responsibilities, duties and the standard of performance expected of them. They also must be clearly warned that their performance is deficient and told in what way it is deficient. Finally, except for gross misconduct, the warned employees must have an opportunity to improve or defend themselves.

Apart from legal aspects, you also have to consider the effects of disciplinary action or dismissal on the rest of the workforce and yourself. Dismissal can cause great stress for all concerned, including yourself. It is important that you are sure in your own mind that you are taking the right action. Unless the dismissed employee was particularly popular, or an informal leader, the effects are not likely to be disruptive to your workforce. However, if you currently feel that you are getting into a situation where you may decide to dismiss a member of staff – or make several redundant – make sure that you are not leaving yourself open to charges of unfair or constructive dismissal. (See *The Barclays Guide to Managing Staff for the Small Business* or obtain booklets from ACAS or the Employment Department – see p. 160 for addresses.) If your procedures were seen to be fair and if you had good cause for taking the step you took, then you will often find that you actually have the support of the workforce. You might even experience a temporary lift in performance.

Finally, having financially analysed your position with respect to your changing capital requirements and determined your new staffing requirements and organization, you should be in a better position to manage any ailing products with regard to both your current situation and your future plans. By applying the same financial criteria (costs, benefits, expected revenue, etc.) to your older products as you would in evaluating new capital investments, including taking into account the wider staffing and organizational implications, you should be able to decide when to start running down outmoded versions of your products – whether goods or services. How to manage a declining product and to move away from it without disrupting your business has been discussed thoroughly in chapter 7 (pp. 113–17) but you should also be aware that your older products can be used to improve your positive cash flow, which will offset the possible early negative cash flow of newer products.

In general, products consume development and support costs in larger quantities when they are young than when they are closer to the end of their life cycles. Indeed, it is common for costs to exceed revenues for some time after launch but, with no money spent on development or promotion and production at a minimum, costs can be at rock bottom by the time the product is due to be withdrawn. Furthermore, if the declining product still requires servicing or spare parts, it is fairly common practice to increase significantly the prices of those goods or services to captive customers who still use your product. This process of *price skimming* is aimed at increasing productivity or profitability without increasing volumes, and should provide you with development funds for some of your more promising potential new products.

Of course, this is another reason why your planning for future growth will need to take into account not only future streams of cash from individual products or services but also their effects on the total cash flow, revenue and profits of your business. Moreover, you will need to monitor constantly the usage of supplies and machines by the changing mix of new and old products, as well as by the people involved in producing and selling them. Supplies can be halted (thus representing a potential cost saving), machines used in connection with the redundant product have to be evaluated, especially if they are also used for producing other products or services (in service firms, computers or reprographic equipment could fall into this category), and your overall requirements from your premises will need to be reassessed regularly. As the next two sections outline, these types of decisions about capital, labour and final products will become increasingly common as the full effects of new technology and the Single Market begin to work their way down to the smaller businesses.

Introducing information technology

New technology is certainly exciting and seems ideal for small growing businesses. It can make existing products cheaper and render competitors' products obsolete tomorrow. The instant transmission of information by electronic means – information technology – has transformed manufacturing industries (offering small firms the chance to compete with large firms but also, paradoxically, encouraging large firms to compete with small firms) and altered the world of financial services out of all recognition. Entire service industries have grown up to support and service the various aspects and applications of information technology. Information technology – in the form of computers, digital mini-switchboards, answering machines, fax machines, and so on – certainly has the power to transform the central and production functions of most small service, distribution or manufacturing businesses.

Although many of these issues are covered in *The Barclays Guide to Computing for the Small Business*, it is worth while summarizing some of the main benefits that computers and other applications of information technology can offer a growing business. For a start, communications in general and the transmission of business documentation in particular have been speeded up enormously. The rapidly increasing use of fax machines and mobile telephones has transformed the sales and delivery functions not only of most services but also small manufacturers and distribution businesses. However, it is usually in the advantages that computers offer to your central administrative functions that computers really shine. For instance, in chapter 6 it was pointed out that growing businesses need to keep very firm control over their invoicing, stock and debtor positions. There are dozens of off-the-shelf programs designed specifically for smaller businesses which will allow you to keep instant track of your invoices, stock items and slow payers. Some of the elements of financial planning were discussed in the previous section (and in chapter 6) and, once again, plenty of financial packages are commercially available. Perhaps the most widespread use of computers in smaller businesses, however, is in the word-processor and database filing of customers, suppliers and general business contacts. Direct mailouts and speedy replies to urgent letters are now well within the capacity of even the busiest of growing businesses – provided your business has the skills available to make proper use of the equipment (or the time available to learn).

With all its advantages, it must be recognized that information technology also imposes an extra burden on small business owners and poses a constant threat to certain small businesses. The burden is increased by the need to keep up with the latest developments in your field through fear of being swamped or undercut. In fact, some businesses need to set aside funds in anticipation of new information technology. Furthermore, it is not just your office organization or production that can be affected but also your requirements for skilled labour and, indeed, your very premises. Taking premises as an example, buildings are an essential part of your business infrastructure (see chapter 5), critical to business success. The spread of information technology (the handling of data by electronic means) is beginning to highlight the weaknesses of inadequate premises. Naturally, these effects can be seen at their most extreme in organizations that exist for the transference of data – the financial services industry. But every company which uses a desk-top computer to store information confronts the same kind of building problems as the 24-hour global trader.

Building services in larger buildings usually have a limited life span – say up to 25 years – and the services in these mainly older buildings tend to be mechanical (heating, ventilation, air conditioning, plumbing and so on) or electrical (lighting, lifts, office machinery, building plant, and so on). In more modern buildings, services may now also include air conditioning, environmental control, power, data, telecommunications, information networks, specialist lighting and various other electronically controlled facilities. To meet the demands of many modern firms, especially those in business and financial services, where appearances and the economic use of high-rental space are very important, buildings have to be adapted to your specific needs by means of finishes, partitions, raised floors, suspended ceilings, lighting fixtures, furniture and perhaps ducting and segregated trunking for power, data and telecommunications.

Information technology, of course, affects much more than just building services, but the pressures imposed on buildings by the rate of change in information technology represent a clearly visible example of the more widespread impact of new technology on all spheres of business. Moreover, even though the best-designed buildings are those that are flexible enough to deal with such change, to achieve that flexibility can impose its own business strains. For instance, the staff at Compburo might require individual local control of their work environments, yet the resulting increase in temperature might mean that Compburo has to install a centrally controlled, general cooling system and new fire detectors. Apart from the need for Compburo to present a modern, hi-tech image, the advantages of modern buildings – with their greater capacity for power and data, combined with generous vertical and horizontal distribution capacity – may become apparent and actually lead to longer-term cost savings even though the special features may also cause space constraints. However, extra costs may include the need to introduce new kinds of lighting to be compatible with heavy use of visual display units (VDUs) or monitor screens. Modern, growing businesses do need to keep abreast of the latest developments in information technology, and the older buildings with single, centralized cores simply cannot carry the services to the parts of the building where they are needed, because facilities are now dispersed. However, buildings with the latest facilities do not come cheap – whether you decide to rent or buy.

In fact, at your current stage of growth, the need to make such decisions may seem rather remote but the strains of successful growth may lead you to these decisions about how to accommodate new technology sooner than you realize. Certainly, the concept of intelligent buildings – buildings that service themselves, service you, and service the organization they contain – is normally associated with extreme hi-tech solutions far beyond the needs of small businesses. However, this rather grand-sounding concept boils down to four elements: office automation, advanced telecommunications, building automation and responsiveness to change. Thus, at your current level of development, the real, time-saving benefits of information technology have to be offset against this increase in the complexity of your management tasks but, as your business develops, the benefits of new technology are likely to make it inescapable. Thus, even if your business seems fairly outside or immune to the effects of new technology, your tranquillity is likely to be temporary. Information technology is not an area that can be ducked, because poor decisions based on lack of information can lead to financial losses and later stunt your firms's growth and prevent it reaching your objectives. Indeed, the electronic transmission of data, documentation, messages, information and even money is being actively encouraged by the European Commission as part of its efforts to create the Single Market in Europe. Consequently, you should gauge your own needs not so much by what your local competitors are doing but by how your more advanced European rivals may be using information technology.

The effects of the Single European Market

By the end of 1992, Europe's 20 million or more employers, family firms and self-employed should be struggling with the realities of operating in a single market. For the 320 million consumers of the European Community, this will mean more than just an end to customs formalities. Apart from the physical barriers to trade, technical barriers – including consumer legislation, health and safety regulations, the testing and certification of standards, regulations on food and pharmaceuticals, and so on – are also due to come down. Also, most of your familiar financial and information services are due for fundamental change and unexpected competition. Of course, for different businesses the patterns of opportunities and threats unleashed by the Single European Market will vary enormously. Ultimately, it seems clear that there will be substantial economic growth over all of Europe but that regional differences may increase and, for some industries, the shorter-term effects could be very severe.

On the positive side, European Commission studies suggest that removal of customs formalities and the opening up of public procurement policies should increase the European Community's economy by 0.5 per cent, the liberalization of financial services by 1.5 per cent and economies of scale and distribution by 2 per cent, leading to an overall economic increase due to the Single Market of about 5 per cent. If these projections turn out to be true, the implications for the European Community as a whole include a cut of 6 per cent off inflation and around 1.8 million more jobs leading to a big increase in demand for the goods and services that satisfy the higher-level needs of status, prestige and self-fulfilment.

However, not all predictions are quite so rosy. For instance, it is likely that half a million to one million jobs may be lost in the European Community as the first impact of the changes is felt, and there is some dispute whether any subsequent uplift caused by the benefits will eventually lead to a net increase of 1.8 million jobs. Also, it is widely expected that direct competition, mergers and economic changes will lead to the disappearance of as many as 6 million of Europe's businesses. Of course, many of these will be replaced by more efficient businesses and by businesses better organized and structured to deal with the new conditions of the Single European Market. Indeed, your own business may be destined to be one of these new Euro-businesses. Whatever the future holds for your business on that score, however, it is clear that you can expect more professional competition (sometimes from unexpected quarters) and side-effects from the impact of the Single Market on your main existing customers and suppliers. It also seems likely that the positive effects of the Single Market will not extend equally to every region in Europe and that, currently, no British region is in the top league of potential gainers from the Single Market. If this more gloomy scenario is more accurate, then you can conclude that there will still be plenty of local demand for the goods and services that cater for lower-level, basic needs for some time to come.

Many of these broader effects, however, will affect mainly the more established medium-sized and large firms. It is less clear exactly how new and smaller businesses will be affected. Indeed, if you are already exporting or dealing with Europe – either directly or through clients – you will have formed your own views on the likely effects of the Single European Market on your own firm. It is worth taking note, however, that the European Commission feels that, despite their renowned flexibility, 'very small businesses and self-employed workers will continue to supply a purely local market and that the most vulnerable units will be the medium-sized firms'. Perhaps you can take heart from the fact that most of Europe's businesses are small (roughly 90 per cent have fewer than 50 employees, though most actually have less than 10 employees), and that very few of their owners adopt a professional or trained approach to their management. Therefore, all the material covered in this book and the other Barclays Guides will help you not merely to control your growth but should also prepare you for dealing positively with the Single European Market.

Question 16   Have you made any plans or taken any concrete steps towards preparing for the Single Market?

In general, very few small firms have made many concrete preparations or have even identified the skills needed to cope with the threats and challenges of the Single European Market. However, if your business is in one of the small business industries that are vulnerable to Europe-wide restructuring, you should be at least taking defensive steps, even if you do not intend to expand into other Member States. The vulnerable sectors, where smaller businesses form at least half of the firms, include machine tools and tools, machinery for the food and chemical industries, lamps and lighting equipment, medical and surgical equipment and precision instruments. Also, if superior infrastructural support and supplies of skilled labour concentrate the large electronics and microcomputer components, aerospace and industrial plastics industries mainly in continental Europe, then most small sub-contractors – manufacturing and specialist services – will also need to establish a presence in continental Europe, near the decision-making centres of the larger firms. Consequently, small German, French, Belgian and Dutch manufacturers and business services may enjoy expanding markets. Although this may present new opportunities for small transport and wholesaling firms in most countries, Britain's more innovative and ambitious small firms will have to consider either buying into an appropriate European firm or establishing their own operation in continental Europe – especially if Britain's skilled workers decide to use the Channel Tunnel to commute to better-paid and better-protected jobs. Already, British construction and property development firms are active in Normandy. A wise defensive strategy in an enlarged market may set the stage for more Europe-wide small business cooperation, but British firms may be less accustomed to such a strategy. As the Single European Market becomes a reality, you will need to ask yourself whether you are prepared for either cooperation or competition with businesses from other parts of Europe.

The preferred model adopted by the European Commission is of small firms from different Member States linking up either for one-off projects or on a longer-term basis. In Britain, however, active small-business exporters strongly prefer to use an agent or distributor rather than establish an overseas presence themselves. The key to success lies in finding the right overseas partner (agent or distributor) and having the commitment and confidence to persist in hammering away at the export market. While formal links among the small firms may not seem feasible, the possibility of future Europe-wide, small-firm cooperation could become a valid option as principal/distributor relationships develop into active cooperation between two small firms. The Commission is keen to encourage this type of development through various initiatives, including subsidized trade fairs for related industries, Euro Info-Centres to provide practical information about the Single Market and other Member States and database networks such as BC-Net (designed to put potential partners in contact with each other). Moreover, differences in national small-firm attitudes towards marketing, cooperation, loss of personal control and so on may also cause distinct patterns in national small firm relationships to emerge.

The effects of 1992 may well be beneficial for certain small financial and business services but the dismantling of barriers to financial services, especially in Italy and France, may make it even easier for British investors to invest in successful German, French and Italian small businesses at the expense of similar but less dynamic British firms. Indeed, Europe's future business environment is more likely to be modelled on countries such as Germany, which strongly emphasizes social involvement with top-quality technical training across all jobs (including managers), than on a less structured *laissez-faire* country such as Britain. As the winds of change blow more strongly, other small-business owners will begin to find it more prudent and wise to find out about the newly integrated market but, if you act now, your business will be continuing its planned growth while they are still seeking workable strategies and answers to their problems.

Developing your corporate culture

Having identified your preferred future customer profile and considered the internal and external effects on your business of such powerful influences as the Single European Market and information technology, you should now consider the central issues facing you and your growing business. Throughout this book, we have returned to the same theme: exactly what sort of business do you want your business to become and where do you want to lead it? As your business grows and the number of complex organizational and commercial decisions increases, it will become harder to have an intuitive feel about what courses of action to take. The feeling of a team spirit when your business was young will become virtually impossible to maintain. It is important to encourage a broader type of team spirit, or a corporate culture as it is often termed in larger organizations, for your business if you are serious about future expansion.

At your present stage of growth, it may seem that the development of a corporate culture – which embraces the issues of organization, marketing and premises, as well as business image – is not urgent. However, it is important both internally (in terms of staff motivation and development) and externally (for marketing and future financing) not to lose your sense of identity as a business. Indeed, as your business grows, the need to present a consistently positive image becomes more important yet more difficult, because the overall image is produced not just by you but also by the other people who work in your business. This means not only that you need to be able to articulate your personal goals for the business but also that you need to be able to communicate those goals to your staff in such a way that they become the goals of your entire business.

This raises a number of other issues for you to consider about your own management and leadership styles. In many smaller businesses – especially those that rely on producing one particular product or one type of service – it is common for the owner to take all the major decisions and to tell members of staff which jobs to do and how to do them. This does not mean that such owners are necessarily aggressive or dictatorial but that they naturally employ a *directive* management style. In other businesses, where members of staff have to operate fairly independently of each other – such as in selling or creative jobs – business decisions can be decided after discussion. Management styles can be viewed as a continuum from this latter, more open, people-oriented style where teams decide or managers 'sell' (*participative*) or 'explain' (*consultative*) their ideas and courses of action to more directed and structured, task-oriented styles where managers either encourage (*paternalistic*) or order (*authoritative*) other members of staff.

Without analysing each style in any detail (some of the references at the back of this book cover these issues more fully), it is worth pointing out that each of these styles can be the most appropriate style for certain circumstances and for particular individuals. Indeed, even though most businesses will have a prevalent style, as they grow they probably need to adopt various mixes of styles for different business areas. Each and every business is sufficiently complex to require its own individual analysis of management styles. However, if your goal is to encourage a businesswide team spirit even as you split your business into separate, delegated functions, it is clear that a more people-oriented, participative approach to your key staff is much more likely to deliver the goods. On the other hand, if performance is to be monitored effectively, some degree of direction will also have to be employed.

Consequently, it may be helpful to address some of the leadership issues that relate to the changing nature of your business as it moves up its growth curve. Whatever the prevailing style of decision-making in a business, it is fairly clear that one of the best leadership techniques is that of leading by example. If you tend to adopt a fairly directive approach, you need to demonstrate to your staff that you do have clear objectives and that you are prepared to monitor performance so that you can fairly reward success and discourage failure. Even if you are committed to a supportive style of management, it will not work unless a genuine participative leadership style is adopted at the very top. If participation seems to go against the grain of the organization, supervisors and some workers will not participate in supportive, people-oriented groups, even when a participative style seems objectively attractive.

Indeed, if you have been coping with some of the problems of growth (as outlined in the early chapters), you may have become aware of how difficult it is to get your staff to understand exactly what you want to do and how you want things done. If you have a reasonably professional management style, it will not have taken you too long to realize that communication is a two-way process, and that leadership is much more than a matter of shouting orders. In fact, it is pointless even trying to isolate the 'leader' from the people being led and the task to be performed. This is particularly true in a smaller growing business, where motivation, communication and morale are vital to future success. Of course, if you already operate under a fairly supportive style, or if participation is quite normal in your industry, you will mainly face the problem of effective monitoring to ensure that performance is up to your standards and that your flexible firm is not getting too flabby or lackadaisical. All these concerns and how your business is designed to handle them both depend on the prevalent 'culture' within your business and contribute to the future development of that culture.

At the beginning of chapter 7, it was pointed out that any smaller business that is serious about future growth has to develop more of a customer-orientation than a product-orientation. Of course, each of these basic business orientations strongly reflects both your own attitudes towards business and the mix of staff attitudes, comments and behaviour which can collectively be called the 'culture' of your business. For instance, in Batchjob the production supervisor may represent the views of most members of staff that their main job is to produce standard components for their client more efficiently than anyone else (including the client) and that the future growth of their workplace depends on its capacity limits to produce those components. In essence, the product-orientation of Batchjob firmly rests on what can be called a task-centred culture. Batchjob's owner, who wants to increase the flexibility of production to deal with more varied, small-batch contracts that appeal to more profitable customer segments, faces the external marketing problems of gaining more of this type of contract, and the internal organizational challenge of altering the internal culture that supports product-orientation into one that supports customer-orientation. In chapter 4, it was suggested that a customer-centred culture with genuine delegation may be the appropriate culture for a professionally minded, small, growing business and, if you feel that this is the right path for your business, you need to start fostering that culture before you grow too large.

However, apart from the people-centred culture, there are a number of other, more common business cultures to consider as being appropriate for your business. These roughly correspond to the usual management and leadership styles, and have been described as the *power culture* ('if you don't like working in my firm and doing what I say, get out!'), the *role culture* ('I am the boss and I demand respect') and the *task culture* ('there's no time to sit around talking and thinking, we've got a job to do'). None of them are normally thought to be appropriate for growing businesses because, as their names imply, they tend to stifle expression of individual talent or imagination when it runs counter to the bounds of the culture. However, each of these cultures is common among smaller (and many not so small) businesses, and would need to be eradicated if the aim is to build a dynamic, flexible structure capable of handling future growth.

Without going too deeply into describing each of these cultures, it is important to point out that many small businesses start off life with a power or task culture. Some of these businesses can be very successful but very few of them grow beyond one to two dozen employees. What is more, many never develop more than one product and their fate is tied to the life cycle of that product. If you are serious about growth you have to think beyond one single product and encourage all members of the workforce to become involved in the life of your business. The knowledge that the business has a mission and a vision of its future, plus a meaningful place for every employee, is an attainable goal for a small firm. It is also an unbeatable employee motivator and an exciting goal for any small business leader.

Of course, at the heart of any attempt to construct a prevailing culture within your business that encourages hard work, attention to quality and a strong sense of commitment, lies the genuine scope that your staff have for feeding their ideas into your decision-making process and receiving recognition for the contribution that they have made. In other words, the development of a corporate culture depends on your system of staff incentives, the capacity of your business to satisfy the higher-order motivational needs of your staff and your own capability for framing your business objectives in terms broadly acceptable to most of your staff. Incentives were discussed in chapter 4 where it was pointed out that the basis for the successful motivation of your workforce depends on your ability to link each employee's performance to the likely satisfaction of a personal work goal.

Financial and non-financial incentives – such as praise, additional, non-wage benefits and career development through training and promotion – will boost motivation and performance, if they satisfy personal work goals and if they are not seen as substitutes for fair pay. Indeed, the development of a sound corporate culture goes beyond maintaining a reasonable system of incentives. You also have to avoid disincentives. It is crucial that you avoid poor work conditions or inadequate job specifications relevant to personal skills because these will act as de-motivators and produce lower perform-ance. The process of creating a collective or team spirit, however, involves more than gathering together a collection of individual preferences.

You have to make a positive attempt to weld your existing staff and newcomers into a group. This means that you certainly need to provide notice-boards and, if you are already familiar with infor-mation technology and have the capacity, you could consider intro-ducing a regular news-letter to facilitate communication amongst everyone working in your business (including yourself). You will also need to pay close attention to staff development, and make sure that it is about more than just acquiring technical skills. Training is also about processes and behaviour and, above all, about developing a professional approach towards work. For this reason, management training and development are very important, either for yourself, for your key staff or for any fairly inexperienced people whom you promote into responsible jobs.

Your overall aim should be to create a generalized professional approach and positive attitudes and practices towards ensuring high quality and responsible delivery of your goods and services. This means, therefore, that you and your managers need to keep up to date with changing legislation and work practices, as well as have an understanding of what goes on in other parts of your business, so that you and they can communicate and pull together as a team. Managers must be prepared for greater responsibility and you should provide access to training to make sure that they are. Training and development go from the bottom to the top and help to ensure that the right person is in the right job with the skills and training necessary to do it efficiently – both today and tomorrow.

Finally, your system of monitoring performance must be seen to be fair and appropriate. Of course, the performance of the work-force can be undermined by factors outside your direct control but, as the very survival of your business demands swift attention to the problem, it is essential that you can analyse why performance has fallen off before it begins to affect morale and undermine your attempts to encourage positive attitudes. If you do have a performance problem, try to find out precisely what it was that the individuals were doing or not doing which adversely influenced performance. If the problem was serious enough for you to spend time and effort on clearing it up, your efforts will be helpful in encouraging good practice in the rest of your staff as well as serving as a role model of how to tackle tricky problems. To repeat, there is nothing more effective in building up a group than to have the leader personally demonstrating how things should be done.

In fact, this last point holds true of your whole approach towards developing a growth strategy. If you are clear about what you want your business to be doing and your staff can see that you are actively putting your ideas into practice, you are more than halfway towards developing the right sort of corporate culture, and you are also a long way towards carrying your staff with you as you plan your future growth. If it is clear to the other people in your business – and to many unseen customers outside your business – that you can identify your growth products and work to satisfy the needs of well-defined customer segments, it will be seen that you are running a well-managed business. Indeed, it should not be too long before the growth of your business becomes not only a clear success but, more importantly, a positive pleasure.

Summary

This chapter has attempted to put your business and its growth into its business context, making sure that you view your business in relation to your external competitive environment and the internal changes that past and future growth brings. The major external influences associated with technological change and the Single Market have been described and their main effects on new and small businesses have been analysed. Finally, as the business grows beyond your immediate grasp, the need to maintain the personal touch by creating a corporate culture has been raised.

Key points

- Keep ahead of your competition by developing a strong customer-orientation.
- Maintain a suitable portfolio of products at various stages of development.
- Adjust your organization, capital equipment and staffing to suit your current and future business prospects.
- Take into account the likely effects of computers and information technology on your future business plans.
- Do not ignore either the direct or the indirect effects of the Single Market in planning your future growth.
- Maintain the unity of your business by developing a corporate culture that encourages positive attitudes towards quality and growth.

9

Removing future uncertainty through planning

This final chapter, which draws on the ground covered in the previous chapters, is to help you develop a plan for your future growth. In many ways this will be similar to your business plan except that it is more of a brief summary of your future intentions and the likely key decisions that you will have to make as your business expands. Indeed, many of the items in your growth plan will reflect the analysis that you conducted in the previous chapters of this book. For instance, the review of your organizational needs leads logically to the identification of your future skills and work-force needs and your likely requirements for training, development and, perhaps, recruitment.

Once you have identified your likely future needs in relation to staffing issues you will be in a position to address your future premises needs. At the same time, you must address various issues connected with the introduction of computers and information technology, especially how this new equipment may transform your financial records and analysis. All these issues imply the need to review your policy towards training – for vocational, technical and management skills – and to start to make systematic use of training – both in-house and elsewhere. Finally, you need to look at more strategic issues, such as new product development, the effects of likely changes to your external business environment, areas that you may diversify into and, most importantly, how you can develop a strong corporate image. In addition, the chapter examines how you can use some of these summaries to monitor and adjust your business targets. The following sections summarize these issues.

Identifying preferred directions

Now that you have completed the book (and even if you have skimmed through parts of it), it is time to return to the questions posed at the beginning. Look once again at your reply to question 6 in chapter 2 on your broad, longer-term goals. After the various issues that you have considered during this book, is your reply still the same? Which do you prefer as your *most* important goal: to develop into a large business, to reach a reasonable size, to be able to afford a comfortable standard of living, to be wealthy, to support a particular lifestyle? Of course, there are many more alternatives but the reason for posing the questions remains the same. Successful management of business growth requires a clear focus on the shorter-term business objectives that will ultimately lead to your longer-term personal goals.

This book has given you an opportunity to analyse and reflect on most of the key areas of your business and, indirectly, on the business environment in which you operate. By now, you should certainly have a reasonable idea about how to identify any of the problems that growth may have brought to your business and how to overcome them. Your future direction as a business, however, does very much depend on your own personal business objectives.

Look at Exhibit 9.1, the 'New directions review grid', and list your personal business objectives in column 1. In column 2, alongside each personal goal, list the corresponding business objectives that you feel will enable you to achieve that personal goal. Under these, list any remaining business objectives, take note of any repetitions and then try to link your various business objectives to your personal goals. In the third column, list any discrepancies between your personal and business objectives plus any reasons for the conflicts between the two (if these exist). The main purpose of this exercise lies in the fourth column, where you should list the actions you feel you should take to reconcile your personal goals with your business objectives, and the actions that you feel need to be taken if your goals are to be achieved. Finally, in column 5, set appropriate deadlines by which you intend to have completed each action in column 4.

The aim of the new directions review is not so much to outline a plan of action as to help you think about your business goals in operational terms that are attainable and in terms that are compatible with your overall personal goals. Therefore, how you think about your own objectives and how you choose to phrase them are not particularly important as long as they are consistent and make sense.

1 Personal goals	2 Business objectives	3 Discrepancies	4 Action	5 Deadline

Exhibit 9.1 New directions review grid

Facilities for the future

Once you are satisfied that you have identified fairly accurately your likely minimum and maximum business development paths over the next five years (as you currently perceive them), you will be in a position to forecast your likely staffing, equipment and premises needs. Of course, the links between your use of new machines and your staffing requirements are very complex and the balance between the two will inevitably change several times during the course of the coming five years.

On one hand, new machines and applications of new technology require certain skills and people for their successful operation, so the introduction of additional new equipment will lead to an increase in staff and the demand for more technical skills (especially if you do not have existing staff with the exact skills). On the other hand, modern machines – both on the factory floor and in many service businesses – are frequently a substitute for labour, so your staffing requirements may actually drop (especially if the new machines are replacing older machines). Reviews of your future staffing, skills and training requirements are the subjects of the next two sections.

In this section, the likely future needs of your business for physical facilities – premises, new technology, machines – are addressed. However, because staffing and facilities requirements are strongly linked, it may help you to refer to chapter 4 (especially the first two sections) and to chapter 5, pp. 77–9, on the efficient use of space. Also, it may be helpful to make sure that your likely future staffing requirements are kept in mind by returning to this review after you have completed the Organizational review grid in the following section.

In Exhibit 9.2 Facilities review grid, list the main functional areas in your business (administrative, sales, supplies, production, and so on) in the first column. Alongside each functional area in column 2, list the equipment and space currently used in that area and, in column 3, the equipment and space required by that area according to your plans for the future. In column 4, list the additions and proposed cost for each item and in column 5 list the disposals and expected sales price of any items. Finally, in column 6 list when you expect to have your new equipment in place.

It may help you to refer to chapter 8, pp. 125–36 and chapter 5 when completing this grid. The information that you list in columns

1 Function	2 Present facilities	3 Future facilities	4 Purchases	5 Sales	6 Deadline

Exhibit 9.2 Facilities review grid

4, 5 and 6 can be more meaningfully summarized in the final summary grid on p. 157 and in your cash-flow forecasts after you have decided whether your expected future revenues justify the changes. Offsetting any receipts from sales of old stock, premises or equipment against expenditure on new facilities, will give you some idea of the scale of revenue (if you also take into account the costs of your proposed staffing changes identified on pp. 53–59) that you will need to break even after each target deadline.

Reviewing your organizational needs

Growth in staff is usually the most obvious outward sign that a business is growing and, if you intend to continue growing, you will need to employ yet more people. Of course, as you grow, the type of people and the skills they have will become increasingly important. Nevertheless, people are a business's most valuable asset and they should be treated accordingly.

You need to address the issues of recruitment and training as well as motivation for your present and future staff. Other things being equal, your main organizational aim should be to develop an effective structure to handle the strains of growth and to get the best out of your staff, by keeping them involved and giving them a chance to grow with your business. You have already identified the main areas of your business that require reorganization, in chapter 4, but you may well have modified your earlier assessment in the light of the material in subsequent chapters.

In the first column of Exhibit 9.3, the Organizational review grid, list your main priorities for new skills or reorganization. In the next column, note the level of authority or job title alongside each skills need and, in the third column, note whether the postholders will be in charge of their own separate budget. In column 4, note whom the postholders will be reporting to, and in column 5 list the people for whom the postholders will be accountable. Finally, in column 6, note the proposed dates by which the skills or the staff need to be in place.

Once you have completed this organizational grid, you should list the order of priority for getting each organizational issue dealt with (this will basically be reflected in the deadlines set in column 6). Next, on the basis of the information that you have recorded, you

1 Skills needs	2 Status	3 Budget?	4 Reporting to	5 In charge of	6 In place by

Exhibit 9.3 Organizational review grid

should try to draw a chart (Exhibit 2.1 on p. 21 gives examples) that reflects your final organizational structure after all the positions have been filled. Of course, as you continue to grow, you should conduct this summary exercise at regular intervals and review your priorities, especially when your organizational charts begin to look rather unwieldy.

Reviewing your training needs

Having established your current and future staffing, skills and organizational needs, you next need to turn your attention to how you intend to acquire the necessary people or skills. Of course, some of the skills will have to be bought in and the processes of recruitment were mentioned in chapter 4 and covered extensively in *The Barclays Guide to Managing Staff for the Small Business*. However, because of the reasons covered in the sections on motivation (pp. 64–70) and on developing your own corporate culture (pp. 143–8), you will need also to introduce training on a systematic basis to provide yourself with the necessary skills, and your staff with reasonable career or development paths.

The main types of staff training and development include training for the immediate practical and technical skills (learning to use a lathe, computer, EPOS till, etc.) and, especially as you grow to a reasonable size, induction training about your business. However, you or your staff may express a need for refresher courses to bring skills up to date. You may need to train for new technology, including adapting existing skills to cope with new equipment, processes or systems. There can be a wide choice of training venues. The training can be carried out on the business premises, either on or off the job, utilizing either your own trainers or outside trainers. Training can also be conducted externally at a college or university during business hours, or at some other third-party premises by outside professionals. Training and development should not be restricted to non-managerial staff.

In column 1 of Exhibit 9.4, the Training review grid, list the areas that you have identified as being suitable for training or where you have identified a skills need. In column 2, list the levels of skills that you need (elementary, awareness, technical competence, independent judgement, management, etc.). Classify the levels of skills in terms that are relevant for your business and the skills in question. In column 3, note the expected numbers of people involved and frequency of training (one-off, a few times a year, regular groups, etc.). In column 4, write the time, location and type of training (Thursday mornings in-house, Monday and Wednesday evenings at a local college, day release at a specialist training centre, distance learning over three weeks, etc.). In column 5 write the expected cost of each item of training and, in column 6, note in money terms the expected gains (include obvious output measures and also expected increases in productivity and efficiency). Finally, think through any major discrepancies between columns 5 and 6 and amend any of the entries in the other columns (or cancel the proposed training, if totally uneconomic) before making sure that the total of column 5 does not exceed the total of column 6.

The total cost in column 5 will form the basis for your training budget although you will also have to include any administrative costs and some costing to account for the time of any other staff involved (for instance, on-the-job instructing, covering for colleagues away at training, etc.). You will have to work out your own logical flow of training activities based on your business priorities and the need to minimize disruption.

1 Area of need	2 Skills level	3 Frequency	4 Training	5 Cost	6 Benefits

Exhibit 9.4 Training review grid

Setting future business targets

Planning the future growth path for your business is not a static process but a dynamic one which requires constant monitoring and adjustments to your business. Exhibit 9.5 Business objectives grid, which is a summary of all the grids that you have completed in the previous sections of this chapter, should be updated periodically. Indeed, if you are finding that any particular areas of the grid need frequent attention, you should return to the primary grid in the appropriate section above.

1 Objectives	2 Facilities	3 Staffing	4 Skills level	5 Priorities

Exhibit 9.5 Business objectives grid

In the first column, list the objectives that you identified as the outcome of the New directions review grid. Next, in column 2, list the facilities, identified in the Facilities review grid, that you believe you will need to achieve each objective. Mark those facilities that will be used to meet more than one objective and the target deadlines for acquiring any new facilities. Complete a similar list in column 3, using the Organizational review grid, for the staffing that you will need to achieve each objective, noting multiple uses of staff and expected deadlines by which staff will be in place. In column 4, with reference to the Training review grid, note any special skills or training needs, and in column 5 note your preferred order of priority for the objectives.

This grid, and the other grids in the previous four sections, should help you work out an order of priorities for using and acquiring resources to attain your objectives. You should find it even more helpful to sketch out a flow chart with target dates so that you can plan your growth in an orderly fashion. Finally, you will need to calculate cash-flow forecasts and projected profit and loss statements so that your future growth does not take you by surprise (see *The Barclays Guide to Financial Management for the Small Business*).

Summary

The main intention of this final chapter has been to provide you with an instrument for monitoring your growth and anticipating key growth decisions. Consequently, it is important to note that none of the information that you gather to complete this plan should be regarded as permanent. Indeed, the plan may look very neat and slick and it may seem that you have overcome the problems that unplanned growth brought you. However, it is essential that you gather fresh information before making any major decision and that you are prepared to scrap your previous plan if you come up with different answers. Remember, to control growth you must be prepared but you must also be flexible.

Key points

- Review your personal goals regularly and make sure that your business objectives fit in with them.
- Conduct periodic reviews of your actual usage of and future needs for all facilities – equipment, machines and premises.
- Regularly monitor your staff – not only in terms of their performance but also in terms of your skills needs.
- Institute a proper programme of training and staff development.
- Set out your growth priorities systematically, according to your current resources, expected revenue flows and likely profits.

Appendix: Sources of Information

Advisory Conciliation and Arbitration Service (ACAS)
Clifton House, 83–117 Euston Road, London NW1 2SH.
Tel.: 071 388 5100
Provides information on disciplinary and dismissal procedures.

Association of the British Chambers of Commerce
Sovereign House, 212 Shaftesbury Avenue, London WC2H 8EW.
Tel.: 071 240 5831
Provides contact telephone numbers and addresses of local Chambers
of Commerce plus a number of advisory leaflets on various business
problems including employment, premises and exporting.

Business in the Community
227a City Road, London EC1V 1LX.
Tel.: 071 253 3716
Provides contact telephone numbers and addresses of local Enterprise
Agencies plus advisory leaflets on various business problems
including financial and marketing issues, employment and premises.

Commission for Racial Equality
Elliot House, 10–12 Allington Street, London SW1E 5EH.
Tel.: 071 828 7022
Provides information on racial and equal opportunity issues in relation
to employment and recruitment.

Confederation of British Industry (CBI)
Centrepoint, 103 New Oxford Street, London WC1A 1DU.
Tel.: 071 379 7400
Provides general business information and a number of booklets on
specific small business problems.

Employment Department
Caxton House, Tothill Street, London SW1H 9NF.
Tel.: 071 273 3000
Provides a range of advisory booklets and consultancy schemes
through the Small Firms Service (Tel.: FREEPHONE ENTERPRISE).
Among the more helpful booklets are: *Fair and Unfair Dismissal:*

a guide for employers; employment legislation booklets; *Individual Rights of Employees: a guide for employers*; *The Law on Unfair Dismissal: guidance for small firms*.

Equal Opportunities Commission
Overseas House, Quay Street, Manchester M3 3HN.
Tel.: 061 833 9244
Provides information on gender and equal opportunities issues in relation to employment and recruitment.

Health and Safety Commission
Baynards House, 1 Chepstow Place, Westbourne Grove, London W2 4TF.
Tel.: 071 229 3456
Provides advice and a range of useful booklets on health and safety regulations in relation to premises, employment and organization of work. Among the more helpful booklets are: *Essentials of Health and Safety* (1988), and the Law of Health and Safety at Work leaflets, including *Essential facts for small businesses and the self-employed*.

Institute of Personnel Management
IPM House, 35 Camp Road, Wimbledon, London SW19 4UX.
Tel.: 081 946 9100
Provides advice and written material on all aspects of personnel and employment.

Industrial Marketing Research Association
11 Bird Street, Lichfield, Staffordshire WS13 6PW.
Tel.: 0543 263448
Provides information on marketing research available to local customers and consumers, market shares and price structures of different markets, plus a directory of research firms and consultants.

Industrial Society
Peter Runge House, 3 Carlton House Terrace, London SW1Y 5DG.
Tel.: 071 839 4300
Provides information, advice and publications on various aspects of business, as well as on training in a number of key business areas.

Market Research Society
15 Northburgh Street, London EC1V 0AH.
Tel.: 071 490 4911

Supplementary Reading

Social Skills and Work by M. Argyle (Methuen, London, 1981). Useful outline of the theory and practice of interpersonal skills in work and organizational settings.

How to Make the Transition from Entrepreneurship to a Professionally Managed Firm by E. G. Flamholtz (Jossey-Bass, London, 1986). A very useful guide through the transitional stages of growth and an outline of the different management styles appropriate to each stage.

Opening the Single Market by C. Gray (Open University, Milton Keynes, 1990). A guide to analysing business strengths and weaknesses in relation to the opportunities and threats of the Single Market, and a step-by-step account of how a small business plans a sensible Single-Market strategy.

Managing the Growing Business by C. Gray and P. Burns (Open University, Milton Keynes, 1990). Introductory module to the Small Business Programme. An overview of the problem of a growing small business and a guide to the distance-learning modules of the Small Business Programme that are appropriate to the particular problems of each individual business.

How to Choose Business Premises by D. Green, B. Chalkley, and P. Foley (Kogan Page, London, 1986). An invaluable help in selecting appropriate premises and in arriving at the best 'lease, buy or refurbish' decision.

Understanding Organisations by C. B. Handy (Penguin, London, 1985). A readable overview of some of the main theoretical and practical aspects of business organizations – including motivation and management styles.

Small Firms Risk Capital Guidebook & Source Directory by D. Purdy (Small Business Research Trust, London, 1988). A very practical analysis of the different mix of small firms' financial requirements and how best to satisfy them.

The Small Business Programme Handbook (Paul Chapman, London, 1990). A useful guide to advice, advisers and help for growing small firms.

Glossary

active tasks Tasks and activities initiated by the doer, as opposed to *reactive tasks*, which are conducted by the doer in response to an external change.

ARCE Average return on capital employed.

cash book Daily record of your cash transactions – whether by credit card, cheque or cash.

cash cows Older, established, more mature products that continue to offer reasonable revenue streams with little need for further development costs.

critical incidents analysis An examination of the sudden or persistent crises which you have to deal with, looking into why your present system broke down, why your presence was required to deal with them, what the cause was, and how frequently such incidents occur.

debentures Legal documents in which the terms and conditions of loans are written.

dogs Products which absorb high development costs without yield or reasonable revenue stream.

80:20 An oft-quoted formula which points out that 80 per cent of your sales comes from around 20 per cent of your customers.

equity A form of direct investment whereby investors acquire rights to dividends and voting rights.

fixed charge A legal charge made as security on specific assets in the business.

floating charge A legal charge over all the assets in the business at any point in time.

gearing/leverage Relationship between the amount of share capital and the amount of loan capital, expected by lenders.

indicator   Used in analysing your key results, indicators are instant measures of effective or ineffective performance, such as sales, profits, customer orders, enquiries, loads, machine output, ratios of total sales, ratios of costs.

key results area   An area central to your business, capable of being improved, and capable of being measured in some way, such as productivity, cost control, personal production, unit production, profitability, sales turnover, orders, contracts, customer enquiries.

margin   The difference between your revenue from sales and the direct costs of those sales.

MOR   Management by objectives and results. A system of management applicable if there is a means for measuring performance and a general agreement in advance that the targets set are reasonable.

overheads   The indirect costs that you incur in keeping the business running (administration, rent, maintenance).

overtrading   A situation in a growing company when you are paying your outgoings faster than you are collecting your incomings.

payback   Break-even on the purchase costs of the investment.

preference shares   Shares paid out at a fixed rate before the ordinary investors are paid their dividends.

price-skimming   Increasing the price of declining goods with the purpose of increasing profitability without increasing volume.

problem children   Products or services which eat up development and promotional costs but do not generate much revenue.

product-gap analysis   A simple analysis which will enable you to see which of your products and markets are your strong points and which look weak.

purchases day-book   A book recording separate, detailed daily records of any purchases, including VAT.

purchases ledger   A record of your suppliers and creditors, with details of outgoing payments and purchases.

ROCE   Return on capital employed.

roles and missions Terms used to describe the nature and scope of work to be done, why the organization exists and what resources it will commit to making it happen.

sales day book A book recording separate, detailed daily records of sales, including any VAT.

sales ledger A book recording each account customer on a separate page, with information about customer's addresses, phone numbers, banking branch, terms of sale and any credit limits, and which also notes dates and details of each sale and of each payment.

soft loan Loans which have rates of interest below base rate.

space audit Measurement of total internal usable space, marking off dead areas such as stairwells, cupboards, passages and toilets, and dividing the remaining space by the number of people using each room.

space budget Total amount of floor space you require, taking into account the work area per person, ancillary areas and secondary circulation areas.

stars Products or services which have both a high-market share and a high growth potential.